ASATRU BOOK OF _____

MW00901141

RUNE EDITION

Table of Contents

Foreword

I arrived late to Midsummer in the Sierras 2012 and the first person I came across was Brad Taylor-Hicks, whom I consider to be a good friend. I was delighted to see him after such a long and arduous drive from Oklahoma to California. After a hug and the fine pleasantries of the greeting, he offered a beer. I caught Stephen McNallen just as he was headed away from the fire to retire after a day just as long and hard as mine had been, and he joined us. As we collected ourselves and took a seat by the fire I spoke to Brad about the need for Asatru to have a collection of daily meditations. So he said "Do it." At first I kind of thought I'd let my rather large mouth overload my little butt yet once again. But I kept it to myself and spent the weekend in the Sierras enjoying the company of many fine folk.

Over the course of the next few days, I engaged in conversation after conversation, focused on who the folk in attendance were and why they were there. Their life experiences ran the gamut. There was a therapist who had a smile on her face the whole time and was assured of the positive aspects of the Nine Noble Virtues in her life as well as in the lives of those she could help; there were former officers and soldiers of our armed services whose mission today is far clearer than orders they had received in the past; there were men who had made mistakes and served time to pay for them. Above all I noticed that these people had been through something that made them look hard enough, or open their eyes enough, to see this way of life and grab a hold of it with all the desperation of the drowning in search of a handhold. Here was a nice cross section of the people in the AFA. There are many, many more members on the internet, a good many of whom I know. I collected the stories and the discussions, and there they sat in the back of my mind, waiting.

One of the main reasons I made the arduous trek to Midsummer in the Sierras was that after having read the sagas, and book after book with the same stories in them, I began to feel as if I were stagnating. Never mind that more often than not a walk in the forest or a day's work on the farm, in the sun and amidst nature, would clear my mind and put me in touch with the divine as I perceive it. Then the various Gods and Goddesses would speak to me of the romance and excitement of life once again. But it seemed as if the drudgery and struggle were beginning to wear me down.

Setback after setback no longer seemed like opportunities. Feeling isolated as a solitary practitioner of our faith, I was no longer growing spiritually. I had always felt that the ability to keep the Nine Noble Virtues and the ideas of the Aesir and Vanir at the forefront of our thoughts would help us push through. But the solid belief I held in myself; and the confidence that I was born with everything I ever needed to survive, thrive, and grow; was beginning to wane. There was a definite need to recharge the batteries.

But still I hadn't put all the pieces together until my girlfriend Stephanie made just an offhand comment about all the bugs on the windshield. She said, "I don't see how you can stand it." And then it all fell into place in one of those silly analogies that mean so much to those who are indeed suffering. As we move through each day we are hit by countless little things that force us to make decisions, or situations in life that are stressful; not all of them bring a smile to our face like the birth of child or a new friend. Some are very hard indeed – the loss of a loved one or of a job or your home. All of which had occurred in my life in the last year. It seemed as if life was getting larger and I was at a loss as to where I could find encouragement in the lore. I had lowered my head and put one foot in front of the other with the resolution that there would be no stopping me. But it was getting damn tough to follow through. So when Stephanie made that comment, I saw how it applied to much more of my life than the bugs on the windshield. As we step further and further away from the spiritual aspect of being, as we knuckle down to get the job done, we lose a little of our spirituality. We lose our sense of balance and our center in life. I find that I become a little more calloused with each "bug on the windshield" until it requires a huge effort to get it all cleaned up. Now the conversation Brad and I had took on a new meaning and a new importance. Another comment I heard was, "They come in and are all gung ho for a little while and then they just fall away." Failure to enlarge upon a spiritual life will almost certainly ensure failure overall. This book is a way to help us all keep the very important ideas of faith at the forefront of our lives on a daily basis.

Bryan Wilton

27 Jun 2012

Sources

I dove into our lore seeking support for my efforts and daily life, and came up with a number of passages that were meaningful to me. These passages, with my thoughts on them, form this Book of Days. The sources are the following, most of which are in the public domain and may be found on-line:

- The Poetic Edda, translated by Henry Adams Bellows
- The Poetic Edda, translated by A.S. Cottle
- The Germania by Tacitus, translated by A.J. Church and W.J. Brodibb
- The Laxdaela Saga, translatedby Muriel Press 1899
- The Prose Edda, translated by Arthur Gilchrist Broduer
- Egil's Saga, translated by WC Green
- Eyrbyggia Saga,translated by William Morris/Eirik Magnusson
- Grettir's Saga, translated by GH Hight
- Kormak's Saga, translated by WG Collingwood/J Stefansson
- Viga Glum's Saga, translated by Edmund Head
- Njal's Saga, translated by George Dasent
- Saga of Eric the Red translated by AM Reeves NL Beamish and RB Anderson
- Honsa-Thori's Saga, translated by Eric V. Youngquest
- Culture of the Teutons by V Gronbech
- Religion of the Northmen by Rudolph Keyser
- The works of the Emperor Julian the Apostate translated by W. Heinemann

Simple guide to the Runes

- ⊕ Fehu- ᚠ Cattle, Wealth, Luck, Harmingja

- ⊕ Uruz- ᚢ Aurochs, Strength, Primal Power

- ⊕ Thurisaz- ᚦ Thurses or giants, Thor, Wise Warrior

- ⊕ Ansuz- ᚨ Woden, Ancestral God, Breath of inspiration

- ⊕ Raidho- ᚱ Ride or Journey, Live in the now

- ⊕ Kenaz- ᚲ Torch, Knowledge

- ⊕ Gebo- ᚷ Gift Hospitality, Generosity

- ⊕ Wunjo- ᚹ Joy Fellowship of Like Minds

- ⊕ Hagalaz- ᚺ Hail Seed Form of Water, Radical Change

- ⊕ Nauthiz- ᚾ Need Fire, Necessity

- ⊕ Isa- ᛁ Ice, Stillness and Concentration

- ⊕ Jera- ᛃ Year, Harvest in line with right action

- ⊕ Ihwaz- ᛇ Yew, Yggdrasil vertical axis of ascendancy

- ⊕ Perthro- ᛈ Fate or Lot Cup, unknown

- ⊕ Algiz- ᛉ Elk connection with the patterns set forth by the divine.

- ⊕ Sowilo- ᛋ Sun, Success

- ⊕ Tiwaz- ᛏ Justice, Personal Sacrifice, Honor, Warrior

- ⊕ Berkano- ᛒ Birch Goddess, Birth, Growth, Renewal

- ⊕ Ehwaz- ᛖ Horse, Teamwork nd Trust

- ⊕ Mannaz- ᛗ Mankind, Intelligence of the human mind from the divine

- ⊕ Laguz- ᛚ Water or Ocean, collective memory

- ⊕ Inguz- ᛜ Seed, The God Ing within us

- ⊕ Dagaz- ᛞ Dawn, Awakening, Realization of Self

- ⊕ Othala- ᛟ Homeland, Ancestral Lot, Spirit of our Ancestors

NORWEGIAN RUNE POEM

ᚠ Fe
Wealth is a source of discord among kinsmen;
the wolf lives in the forest.

ᚢ Ur
Dross comes from bad iron;
the reindeer often races over the frozen snow.

ᚦ Thurs
Giant causes anguish to women;
misfortune makes few men cheerful.

ᚨ As
Estuary is the way of most journeys;
but a scabbard is of swords.

ᚱ Reidh
Riding is said to be the worst thing for horses;
Reginn forged the finest sword.

ᚲ Kaun
Ulcer is fatal to children;
death makes a corpse pale.

ᚺ Hagall
Hail is the coldest of grain;
Christ created the world of old.

ᚾ Naudhr
Constraint gives scant choice;
a naked man is chilled by the frost.

ᛁ Isa
Ice we call the broad bridge;
the blind man must be led.

ᚬ Ar
Plenty is a boon to men;
I say that Frodi was generous.

ᛋ Sol
Sun is the light of the world;
I bow to the divine decree.

ᛏ Tyr
Tyr is a one-handed god;
often has the smith to blow.

ᛒ Bjarkan
Birch has the greenest leaves of any shrub;
Loki was fortunate in his deceit.

ᛗ Madhr
Man is an augmentation of the dust;
great is the claw of the hawk.
ᛚ Logr
A waterfall is a River which falls from a mountain-side;
but ornaments are of gold.
ᛦ Yr
Yew is the greenest of trees in winter;
it is wont to crackle when it burns.

The inclusion of a brief outline of the runes and the Norwegian Rune Poem, along with a guided rune meditation every other day, was done after the careful consideration of a number of things. For one, they runestaves are a serious, yet vital part of our faith originating from somewhere outside the realm of even the gods. Odin did not create them, he earned them through self sacrifice. That being said, I think it is both prudent and wise to avoid the overuse of these symbols in our life. If we are meditating on a different rune and all the charactersitcs associated with each one every day, there is the distinct possibility your life will begin to resemble a chaotic mess. Change in our life should be taken one step at a time. Consider carefully before you meditate or begin to galdr a rune based upon the daily suggestion. Perhaps you may wish to think upon a rune for an entire week. Please feel free to do so. Become accustomed to what is taking place in the world around you before you move on to the next one. Or, you may feel you have a firm grasp on the situation at hand and feel the need to grow stronger. Do it, become all you can be. Having said all of that, be aware this book is here to help the folk keep and maintain a powerful, healthy focus on our gods and goddesses in our daily life. Write your thoughts down, keep track of your growth and maybe someday, that thought or idea you jotted down, will inspire a president.

Hail The Folk! Hail The Gods!

Snowmoon/January

Industriousness

Helgakvitha Hjorvarthsson 9
The Valkyrie Spake:
"In the hilt is fame, | in the haft is courage,
In the point is fear, | for its owner's foes;
On the blade there lies | a blood-flecked snake,
And a serpent's tail | round the flat is twisted."

If you work in a job or have your own business, or if you engage in a craft or skill, make sure that in all you do, you imbue it with quality worthy of your name. This stanza refers to a sword lying in Sigasholm, the best of all swords, known as shield breaker. I can assure you it wasn't made with anything less than the greatest effort and skill on the part of the blacksmith.

*Meditate on **Dagaz** or dawn and the new day of your exisitence after being forged by the trials of life.*

Notes

Prose Edda
Sindri laid a pigskin in the hearth and bade Brokkr blow, and did not cease work until he took out of the hearth that which he had laid therein. But when he went out of the smithy, while the other dwarf was blowing, straightway a fly settled upon his hand and stung: yet he blew on as before, until the smith took the work out of the hearth.

Do not let a little discouragement dissuade you from your efforts.

Notes

_____

_____

_____

_____

_____

_____

_____

_____

_____

Prose Edda
Next, he laid gold in the hearth and bade Brokkr blow and cease not from his blast until he should return. He went out; but again the fly came and settled on Brokkr's neck and bit now half again as hard as before; yet he blew even until the smith took from the hearth that gold ring which is called Draupnir.

Sometimes our efforts continue to be met with derision or comments that wound us, as if what we are doing isn't worthwhile. Occasionally our own minds will entertain these thoughts and plague us with doubt. See it through, do your best to finish it, and keep your word.

*Meditate on **Isa** or ice as a way to slow things down and focus on them.*

Notes
_____
_____
_____
_____
_____
_____
_____
_____
_____
_____

Grougaldr 4
Groa spake:
"Long is the way, | long must thou wander,
But long is love as well;
Thou mayst find, perchance, | what thou fain wouldst have,
If the fates their favor will give."

Love is an effort that is always well worthwhile. Can you take that extra step to work hard for what you love, be it a spouse, a sibling, a friend, your children, or parents?

Notes
_____
_____
_____
_____
_____
_____
_____
_____
_____

Hyndluljoth 10
Freyja spake:
"For me a shrine | of stones he made,--
And now to glass | the rock has grown;--
Oft with the blood | of beasts was it red;
In the goddesses ever | did Ottar trust."

In the Goddesses did he trust and they loved him for it. His efforts were well rewarded and they remembered him. Industriousness does not always have to apply to manual labor or our jobs. We should be just as industrious when it comes to developing our faith.

Meditate on **Berkano** *or the Birch Goddess as a rune of becoming.*

Notes

Rigsthula 44
But Kon the Young | learned runes to use,
Runes everlasting, | the runes of life;
Soon could he well | the warriors shield,
Dull the swordblade, | and still the seas.

In the Rigsthula, Rig goes around and touches the lives of three couples with the divine. All of them worked hard in the roles they had in their society, but Kon the Young went a step further and worked just as hard with his faith. Have you taken that step to work as hard in your faith?

Notes

_____

_____

_____

_____

_____

_____

_____

_____

_____

_____

Havamol 60
Of seasoned shingles | and strips of bark
For the thatch let one know his need,
And how much of wood | he must have for a month,
Or in half a year he will use.

Working hard is good, but we must always have a goal in mind as to what we are working for. Make sure you plan for what you need; goals are as essential to our success as the work required to achieve them.

*Meditate of **Jera** or year as a rune of harvest of right action.*

Notes
_____
_____
_____
_____
_____
_____
_____
_____
_____
_____

Vafthruthnismol 3
"Much have I fared, much have I found.
Much have I got from the gods;
And fain would I know how Vafthruthnir now
Lives in his lofty hall."

Even after we have achieved what we feel to be our success, it does not mean we should rest on our laurels. Odin demonstrates this to us in his many quests by accepting the challenge of personal development. It is important to note that Odin does not continue his growth because he is forced to do so, but because it is the right thing to do. We should all follow suit.

Notes
_____
_____
_____
_____
_____
_____
_____
_____
_____

Lokesanna 6
Loki spake:
"Thirsty I come | into this thine hall,
I, Lopt, from a journey long,
To ask of the gods | that one should give
Fair mead for a drink to me."

Here we have Loki, representing the uninspired human intellect, demanding to be given that which he has not earned through work or triumph. "Lopt" is a term for fire, a destructive force that consumes all in its path until it eventually destroys even itself. Here he is preparing to do the same thing by insulting the gods and in effect burning his bridges. And we all know what happened to him. If we are thirsty, let us thirst for knowledge and lay the groundwork with planning and goals and the guidance of the lore to lead us to richer fields.

*Meditate on **Othala** or homeland or ancestral divine inheritance.*

Notes

Havamol 59
He must early go forth | whose workers are few,
Himself his work to seek;
Much remains undone | for the morning-sleeper,
For the swift is wealth half won.

Lying around until noon each day is probably not the best way to build the fortune you feel you deserve.

Notes

Voluspa 7
At Ithavoll met | the mighty gods,
Shrines and temples | they timbered high;
Forges they set, and | they smithied ore,
Tongs they wrought, | and tools they fashioned.

The Gods themselves labored to build for them and for us mighty halls to enjoy now and hereafter. We should do our best to emulate that.

*Meditate on **Sowilo** or sun as a rune of success.*

Notes
_____
_____
_____
_____
_____
_____
_____
_____
_____

Rigsthula 22
He began to grow, | and to gain in strength,
Oxen he ruled, | and plows made ready,
Houses he built, | and barns he fashioned,
Carts he made, | and the plow he managed.

The second couple Rig encountered produced a fine son. We see words like fashioned, ruled, and managed for the things the average man needs to do in his daily life. He mastered his crafts and skills to the best of his ability – a fine example for all his progeny.

Notes

Havamol 82
When the gale blows hew wood, | in fair winds seek the water;
Sport with maidens at dusk, | for day's eyes are many;
From the ship seek swiftness, | from the shield protection,
Cuts from the sword, | from the maiden kisses.

If we know when to work, we will know when to expect the best results.
It is also a reminder not to try and get blood from a turnip. There is no
wisdom in wasted efforts to turn lead into gold. Once again proper
planning will open the best ways to demonstrate our abilities as today's
Asatruar by living successful lives.

Meditate on **Ehwaz** *or horse as a rune of teamwork.*

Notes

_____

_____

_____

_____

_____

_____

_____

_____

_____

Allvismal
I alone among Gods am marriage maker.

Thor's mighty powers of destruction in his weapon Mjolnir also represent the power of creation. His statement about being the marriage maker among the Gods is important. If we look closely at his statement and understand his strength, perhaps when we ourselves are challenged in life we may find strength to weather the storm not only in Thor but in the unions he blesses. Perhaps there was more wisdom than we thought in the sanctity of marriage among the peoples of northern Europe. It may have been another source of strength for a strong people. Today we celebrate all these aspects of Thor and invite him to join our feast.

Notes

Hovamol 126
I rede thee, Loddfafnir! | And hear thou my rede,-
Profit thou hast if thou hearest,
Great thy gain if thou learnest:
A shoemaker be, | or a maker of shafts,
For only thy single self;
If the shoe is ill made, | or the shaft prove false,
Then evil of thee men think.

This passage is important and speaks to a basic tenet of human nature. If I am making my own stuff then I have no one to blame but myself if it fails. I take that to mean I should always do my best at whatever I lay my hands on. If I decide to buy something, well then – they have always said let the buyer beware.

Meditate on **Perthro** *or unknown as luck in your life.*

Notes

Grimnismal 20
O'er Mithgarth Hugin | and Munin both
Each day set forth to fly;
For Hugin I fear | lest he come not home,
But for Munin my care is more.

Odins concern of losing Munin over Hugin, memory over thought, is
especially poignant concerning todays effort to recover our past. We
have lost so much with regards to our heritage and we daily do our best to
recover as much of it as we can. Right here in the lore, from so long ago,
we are told of a very good reason to keep our faith alive and use journals
such as this one. Our memories give us a solid foundation to build
rational thoughts and negotiate the path before us.

Notes
_____
_____
_____
_____
_____
_____
_____
_____
_____

Grimnismal 43
In days of old | did Ivaldi's sons
Skithblathnir fashion fair,
The best of ships | for the bright god Freyr,
The noble son of Njorth.

Your finest work brings great credit not only upon yourself but also upon your parents and children. Something worth remembering.

*Meditate on **Laguz** or ocean as our collective memory.*

Notes
_____
_____
_____
_____
_____
_____
_____
_____
_____

Prose Edda
Well know I, Odin,
Where you hid your eye:
In the crystal-clear
Well of Mimer.
Mead drinks Mimer
Every morning
From Valfather's pledge.
Know you yet or not?

A great sacrifice was made by Odin to learn. What sacrifice have you or I made to learn, and earn wisdom? Mimir is in such a postion that he may indulge in the mead of wisdom every day, likewise through Odins pledge, he is also capable of imbiding the sacred waters of wisdom. But unlike Mimir, Odin has given us the capability to learn these things as well. The great measuring stick of personal growth is whether or not it requires a great deal of pain to put that gift into use in our lives.

Notes

_____

_____

_____

_____

_____

_____

_____

_____

_____

Prose Edda

Vidar is the name of the silent Asa. He has a very thick shoe, and he is the strongest next after Thor. From him the gods have much help in all hard tasks.

His good works and mighty deeds spoke well enough of themselves; there was no need to go about bragging on this or that effort. We are our deeds. If they have merit it will be readily apparent to all those around us.

Meditate on **Tiwaz** *or justice concerning our honor.*

Notes
_____
_____
_____
_____
_____
_____
_____
_____
_____

Prose Edda
But how came the Asas by Suttung's mead? Answered Brage: The saga
about this is that Odin set out from home and came to a place where nine
thralls were mowing hay.

Odin uses every trick in the book to obtain Suttung's mead. Are we using
every asset we possess to attain our goals?

Notes

_____
_____
_____
_____
_____
_____
_____
_____
_____
_____

Prose Edda
Wax not Vimer,
Since I intend to wade
To the gards of giants.
Know, if you wax,
Then waxes my Asa-might
As high, as the heavens.

Believe in yourself, even more than others do.

Meditate on **Ehwaz** *and developing trust through teamwork.*

Notes

_____

_____

_____

_____

_____

_____

_____

_____

Prose Edda
At the same time he reached the river bank and got hold of a shrub, and so he got out of the river. Hence the adage that a shrub saved Thor.

Sometimes it is the least of things that are of the most importance; pay attention to the details.

Notes
_____
_____
_____
_____
_____
_____
_____
_____
_____

Prose Edda
But Fafner went to Gnita-heath (the glittering heath), where he made himself a bed, took on him the likeness of a serpent (dragon), and lay brooding over the gold.

It has been said that behind every great fortune is the shadow of a lie. Does our work effort reflect an honest attitude towards business?

Meditate on **Inguz** *or literally seed but also Ing the divine or sacred place for our work to be the work of craftsmen no matter the job.*

Notes
_____
_____
_____
_____
_____
_____
_____
_____
_____

Prose Edda
Frode! You were not
Wary enough,—
You friend of men,—
When maids you bought!
At their strength you looked,
And at their fair faces,
But you asked no questions
About their descent.

When doing business with another person, take the time to find out who they are and the quality of their work. Do not be seduced by flashy ads and fancy promises.

Notes
_____
_____
_____
_____
_____
_____
_____
_____
_____

Eyrbyggja Saga
And at that Thing was one of the holiest of steads, but there men were not
forbidden to go their errands.

The Thing is important, as in this case a great peace had been settled; but
no man should be so foolish as to not make hay when the opportunity
arises.

Meditate on **Sowilo** *or the sun as a rune of success in all our endeavors.*

Notes
_____
_____
_____
_____
_____
_____
_____
_____
_____
_____

Germania
And their generals procure obedience not so much by the force of their authority as by that of their example, when they appear enterprising and brave, when they signalize themselves by courage and prowess; and if they surpass all in admiration and pre-eminence, if they surpass all at the head of an army.

Do you lead by example? This is one of the principles of leadership proven by thousands of years of experience and still in use today. It requires that we always be out front; to do that, we have to work harder than the man next to us. Not only in the skills of a warrior, but also in our ability to communicate effectively, to be well read and to develop ourselves as a well rounded individual. Spiritually, physically, mentally and emotionally.

Notes
_____
_____
_____
_____
_____
_____
_____
_____
_____
_____

Germania

For they strive not to bestow labour proportional to the fertility and
compass of their lands, by planting orchards, by enclosing meadows, by
watering gardens. From the earth, corn only is exacted.

An unfavorable observation by Tacitus concerning the farming aptitude
of the Germanic tribes, but this is relative to his home of Rome and Italy
where even today we get the best of wines. He does say they grow corn,
and if we think about it for just a second we begin to realize that much of
our faith revolves around corn and the harvest. I feel quite sure that it
was a big deal for our ancestors. I cannot be distracted from what I do
because someone else doesn't feel it's as important.

Meditate on **Nauthiz** *or need fire that our efforts don't become distracted.*

Notes

_____

_____

_____

_____

_____

_____

_____

_____

_____

_____

Rigsthula 9

He began to grow,	and to gain in strength,
Soon of his might	good use he made
With bast he bound,	and burdens carried,
Home bore faggots	the whole day long.

Here we have an example of Rig's first effort to provide humanity with a second dose of the divine; in this we see the effort the man places on what he does, even if it is the lowliest of jobs. He does it well and he does it all day long. Do we put that same effort into the simplest of tasks of our daily lives?

Notes

_____

_____

_____

_____

_____

_____

_____

_____

_____

Atlamol en Gronlenzku 8
The noble dames bore mead,
of many things there was abundance,
many horns passed round,
until it seemed they had full drunken.

The efforts of the fairer sex should never be looked down upon or diminished because they are not understood. These are noble dames and their efforts are blessed by Frigga, who knows all and looks over those who manage the hearth. We should all take a little pride in those efforts to run and manage a home.

Meditate on **Othala** *or homeland and all the efforts required to ensure it's cared for.*

Notes
_____
_____
_____
_____
_____
_____
_____
_____
_____
_____
_____

Culture of the Teutons
By virtue of his dominance over nature, man can also combine souls, and engraft the essence of one upon another. Thus he inspires that which his hands have worked on, and equips his implements with qualities calculated to render them useful in their calling.

Having been blessed twice by the Gods as a people, once when we were created and once again when Rig visits, we have some dominion over nature – not to rule over or master it but to utilize it in a way that best supports and encourages our mind, body, and spirit. Else why would it all be here and why would it all be tied together? There are cycles within cycles that we are a part of. Our ancestors had a better understanding of this than we do. Do not scoff; we cannot build a Stonehenge or construct a pyramid. Our faith is one way we can try to more closely align ourselves with the world we live in, if we continue to work at it.

Notes
_____
_____
_____
_____
_____
_____
_____
_____
_____

Germania

Chaucians do not only possess but fill; a people of all the Germans the most noble, such as would rather maintain their grandeur by justice than violence. They live in repose, retired from broils abroad, void of avidity to possess more, free from a spirit of domineering over others. They provoke no wars, they ravage no countries, and they pursue no plunder. Of their bravery and power, the chief evidence arises from hence, that, without wronging or oppressing others, they are come to be superior to all. Yet they are all ready to arm, and if an exigency require, armies are presently raised, powerful and abounding as they are in men and horses; and even when they are quiet and their weapons laid aside, their credit and name continue equally high.

Tacitus observes a tribe worthy of recognition, a confident people with higher ideals in mind. There is no mention of egos or super egos or false egos or whatever you want to call it running out of control. Their efforts were focused on the quality of life – a life which they had worked hard enough at that they were recognized by an enemy. What greater recognition could there be?

Meditate on **Mannaz** *or mankind and the structure of the divine intelligence in our psyche.*

Notes

Horning/February

Justice
_____

Prose Edda
Now Skadi, the daughter of the giant Thjazi, took helm and birnie and all
weapons of war and proceeded to Ásgard, to avenge her father.

Without or with fear we are not told, but her feeling of love and the idea
that justice was on her side enabled her to approach and challenge the
mighty Aesir. If we are doing it right – and by that I mean life – we
should also be able to move forward to accept any challenge with love and
justice on our side.

*Meditate on **Tiwaz** for just victory in our battles.*

Notes
_____
_____
_____
_____
_____
_____
_____
_____
_____
_____

Brot at Sigutharkvithu 2
Gunnar spake:
"Sigurth oaths to me hath sworn,
Oaths hath sworn, and all hath broken;
He betrayed me there where truest all
His oaths, methinks, he ought to have kept."

This was his claim on the hero's life. Do we take the time to carefully consider our oaths? In today's society we typically will not allow the taking of a life for breaking an oath. But somewhere in the back of our minds we know that our lives will have to be led differently if we break an oath. In the breaking of an oath we have made, we have mined the path of our life. Consider carefully what your oath could mean should you fail to keep it. What will it cost you in the long run?

Notes
_____
_____
_____
_____
_____
_____
_____
_____
_____

Grimnismol 2
'Twixt the fires now   eight nights have I sat,
And no man brought meat to me,
Save Agnar alone,   and alone shall rule
Geirröth's son o'er the Goths.

In doing the right and just thing, his aim to simply relieve the suffering of a man in peril, he was greatly rewarded. We may not always receive such a reward, but if we do the right thing to help another we can always stand tall, hold our head high, and take ourselves anywhere a free man may roam. Today I'll do my best to exemplify what it means to do the right thing and set an example for those around me.

Meditate on **Gebo** *concerning our hospitality.*

Notes

Alvissmol
THOR
Words are changeful as the wind,
And never meant a God to bind.

In our look at justice we have a clear statement made by Thor concerning words. All too often we hear of folk discussing how the Gods have broken this or that oath and it would seem to be a lack of justice on their part. But I would submit that the Gods are so far above us that our limited perception of them may not always be correct. Their resources, power, and knowledge of what the future holds are not things we can easily perceive. My point is that we cannot use the examples in the lore as justification to conduct our lives in a manner different from what has been prescribed. We have a responsibility to take our oaths and justice seriously.

Notes

_____

_____

_____

_____

_____

_____

_____

_____

_____

Germania
Affairs of smaller moment the chiefs determine: about matters of higher consequence the whole nation deliberates; yet in such sort, that whatever depends upon the pleasure and decision of the people is examined and discussed by the chiefs.

The foundations of democracy are found here in the ancient north. Not in the halls of stone found Greece and Rome like we've been taught. But in the verdant forests of the hills and mountains of the north of Europe. As such it is our heritage and we should always endeavor to support and encourage it.

Meditate on **Raidho** *or ride, live in the now.*

Notes
_____
_____
_____
_____
_____
_____
_____
_____
_____
_____

Germania
Where no accident or emergency intervenes, they assemble upon stated days, either, when the moon changes, or is full: since they believe such seasons to be the most fortunate for beginning all transactions.

In the seriousness of these gatherings they have chosen the most obvious signs an ancient culture could use. In doing so they may have relied somewhat upon traditions and spiritual guidance. But the possibility exists that the close proximity to nature and an understanding of their place in it played a much more important role in their daily lives than in ours. What can I do to reclaim some of this balance in my own life?

Notes

Germania
It is by the Priests that silence is enjoined, and with the power of correction the Priests are then invested. Then the King or Chief is heard, as are others, each according to his precedence in age, or in nobility, or in warlike renown, or in eloquence; and the influence of every speaker proceeds rather from his ability to persuade than from any authority to command.

The beginning evidence of equality, and rank based upon proven abilities. Here we have an example of "we are our deeds" bearing fruit in a fledgling society, an example that can easily be transferred into today's society. Following the herd of popularity does us no favors in the long run, when it comes time to speak up.

*Meditate on **Alghiz** or elk and our connection with our higher self.*

Notes

_____

_____

_____

_____

_____

_____

_____

_____

_____

_____

Germania
Yet the laws of matrimony are severely observed there; nor in the whole of their manners is aught more praiseworthy than this.

What more worthwhile institution than marriage to demonstrate the power of right action. It is one of the foundations for all we do in life.

Notes
_____
_____
_____
_____
_____
_____
_____
_____
_____
_____

This is a day to remember a noble farmer from Norway who would not renounce his beliefs in the face of adversity. He was tied to a table and a brazier of hot coals was placed upon his stomach until they had burned through to his insides and he literally burst. Who knows what thoughts ran throughhis head amidst the madness to which the pain undoubtedly drove him. But he did not trade his faith for an easier, softer way. We should not either.

While we may celebrate these strong individuals, we should always be on guard against assuming a stance of righteous indignation. Demeaning another person's faith reduces our own spirituality. Set an example others would wish to follow.

Meditate on **Thurisaz** *literally thurses or giants but also it is the wise warrior.*

Notes
_____
_____
_____
_____
_____
_____
_____
_____
_____
_____

Germania
In truth, nobody turns vices into mirth there, nor is the practice of corrupting and of yielding to corruption, called the custom of the Age.

Live life in the manner it was meant to lived, to its fullest. To hike Kilimanjaro requires a lot of effort. Even then they knew the shortcut of a drug-induced high or the seduction of another would never compete with the grand adventure of life and exploration, and those who take the shortcuts to the joys of life should not be respected even today.

Notes
_____
_____
_____
_____
_____
_____
_____
_____
_____
_____

Prose Edda

XXXII. "Forseti is the name of the son of Baldur and Nanna daughter of Nep: he has that hall in heaven which is called Glitnir. All that come to him with such quarrels as arise out of law-suits, all these return thence reconciled. That is the best seat of judgment among gods and men."

The best seat of judgment among Gods and men: We should be aware that to have a God dedicated to the settlement of the law-suit and that his should be proclaimed the "best" seat of judgment speaks volumes as to the importance of justice in the ancient north.

*Meditate on **Kenaz** or torch a symbol of the light of justice.*

Notes

_____

_____

_____

_____

_____

_____

_____

_____

_____

Prose Edda
A hall is called Glitnir, with gold 'tis pillared,
And with silver thatched the same;
There Forseti bides the full day through,
And puts to sleep all suits.

Glitnir has also been noted to be a home for Baldur, who is a sun God or shining God, and it is made of silver and gold. All of these symbols represent purity and the hope a common man may have in a system of justice. Let the truth light the way.

Notes

_____

_____

_____

_____

_____

_____

_____

_____

_____

_____

Prose Edda

The ninth is Vár: she harkens to the oaths and compacts made between men and women; wherefore such covenants are called 'vows.' She also takes vengeance on those who perjure themselves.

We also have one of Frigga's handmaidens focused as it were on taking vengeance upon the oath breaker. A form of her name has survived to this day as "vow."

*Meditate on **Jera** as rune of right action.*

Notes

_____

_____

_____

_____

_____

_____

_____

_____

_____

Prose Edda
He is the wisest of the Æsir, and the fairest-spoken and most gracious;
and that quality attends him, that none may gainsay his judgments. He
dwells in the place called Breidablik, which is in heaven; in that place may
nothing unclean be, even as is said here.

The fine qualities of Baldur cannot be questioned; here Baldur is said to
reside in Breidablik. Vali was the one to avenge Baldur. Let's take a
moment in this feast to honor the God who avenged for us a wrong that
injured the entire world. An argument could be made that we still suffer
from it. Hail the Day-Old God!!

Notes
_____
_____
_____
_____
_____
_____
_____
_____
_____

Prose Edda

The eleventh is Syn: she keeps the door in the hall, and locks it before those who should not go in; she is also set at trials as a defense against such suits as she wishes to refute: thence is the expression, that Syn[denial, refutation]is set forward, when a man denies.

In a time that most of the world views as the Dark Ages, our ancestors held in high regard right action and justice. Indeed there are two Deities for justice alone: Forsetti and Syn. Forsetti never gave a judgment that was not favorably accepted, and Syn is the de facto public defender. This balance of male and female in our system of justice is important in reestablishing the equality and importance of both sexes in our society today.

Meditate on **Jera** *as a rune of right action.*

Notes
_____
_____
_____
_____
_____
_____
_____
_____
_____
_____

Prose Edda

Hárr answered: "In the beginning he established rulers, and bade them ordain fates with him, and give counsel concerning the planning of the town; that was in the place which is called Ida-field, in the midst of the town. It was their first work to make that court in which their twelve seats stand, and another, the high-seat which Allfather himself has."

The Allfather's first order of business, after Asgard was made, was to establish rulers and a court. We cannot overlook the importance of the establishment of the 12-God pantheon as well; we see it repeated time after time in mythologies around the world, and it is mirrored in our own judicial system with its 12-person juries.

Notes

_____

_____

_____

_____

_____

_____

_____

_____

_____

_____

Frisian Law from the time of Charlemagne
If anyone breaks into a shrine and steals sacred items from there, he shall
be taken to the sea, and on the sand, which will be covered by the flood,
his ears will be cleft, and he will be castrated and sacrificed to the god,
whose temple he dishonored.

This passage is usually cited the most when this ancient book of law is
referred to, along with a passage about the killing of children. These laws
had been passed down for generations until Charlemagne ordered them
written down in the Middle Ages.

Meditate on **Laguz** *as a rune of the collective unconscious memory.*

Notes
_____
_____
_____
_____
_____
_____
_____
_____
_____

Prose Edda
Forseti, He is the son of Baldur---of spotless Innocence. When Innocence disappeared from the earth, Righteousness was left behind to fill its place.

One more reason we have to treasure justice as we should and do in our daily lives.

Meditate on **Mannaz** *as rune of mankind and our capabilities.*

Notes

_____

_____

_____

_____

_____

_____

_____

_____

_____

_____

Religion of the Northmen
Drótnar, In the earliest ages this name was peculiar to the highest rulers
of the people, who at the same time presided at the courts of justice and
were high-priests; but it gave way at an early period to konungr (king),
the title of honor which has been customary since.

This term Konungr or a variation of it is used in the Rigsthula. In Rig's
establishment of the nobility, we see originally a class of person who had
the faith of the people and who was entrusted with justice. Through the
ages, positions of rank have morphed many times, depending upon the
state of enlightenment of the attendant people.

Notes

Religion of the Northmen
The heathen North men considered Judicial Proceedings in the main to be closely connected with Religion, and, so to speak, under the direction of the Gods, from whom they imagined all Law and Justice originally proceeded.

This is a fairly clear statement concerning exactly how influential the tribes of Northern Europe considered their Gods and Goddess to be in the most important of arenas: the courtroom. Our challenge today is to do our best to rely upon that same sense of wisdom and justice from the Aesir in our daily life.

*Meditate on **Tiwaz** as a rune of justice.*

Notes

_____

_____

_____

_____

_____

_____

_____

_____

_____

Religion of the Northmen
They also conceive that the Gods, especially in certain legal proceedings,
more immediately made their appearance, either as witnesses or as judges.
Of such proceedings the Oath and the Duel were the most important.

In an oath or a duel the connection with the Gods becomes very clear and
apparent, primarily because our heart is involved. Not our intellect, but
the very well of our bodies is engaged in our actions, if they are pure and
followed through. Our heart or our well of being is filled to overflowing
with either victory, or the reward of an oath fulfilled.

Notes
_____
_____
_____
_____
_____
_____
_____
_____
_____
_____

Landnamabok quoted in The Religion of the Northmen
"A ring of two ounces in weight, or larger, shall lie upon the altar in every chief-temple; this ring shall the priest bear upon his arm at all the assemblies of the people which he shall preside over; and he shall beforehand dip it in the blood of the ox which he himself has sacrificed. Every man who may have a case to be tried before the Court , shall first take oath upon this ring, and name for himself two or more witnesses: 'I call upon these men as witnesses,' he shall then say, 'That I take oath upon the ring , lawful oath, so help me Frey and Njörð and the Almighty Ás (Odin), that I will so prosecute---or defend, or bear witness in, or judge--- this cause in such manner as I know to be most just and true, and most consistent with the law, and that I will fulfill all lawful obligations concerning the cases which I may have to act upon, while I am in this Assembly.'"

In this long paragraph found in the Landnamabok we have a clear outline of the oath administered by the Icelandic heathens. From the size and material of the ring, how it was prepared, and who was to be called – both men and Gods – it becomes very clear just how important the oath was and is in the life of the Asatruar. An oath must follow the law and faith of the person taking it. Common sense tells us breaking either law or faith, will, at the very least lead us into shame and possibly into matters much more serious. While it may be intimidating, living the Nine Noble Virtues allows us to hold our heads high and do the right thing to begin with. We can take honorable oaths with pride.

*Meditate of **Ehwaz** as a rune of teamwork.*

Notes
_____
_____
_____
_____
_____
_____
_____
_____
_____
_____

Religion of the Northmen
"First shalt thou swear me
        All the oaths:---
    By the Ship's deck
    And the Shield's margin,
    By the Steed's neck
    And the Sword's edge,---
    That thou torment not
    The wife of Völund,
    Nor of my bride
    Become the destroyer."

Outside of courts they made use of other oaths, as we find they swore by certain objects which were looked upon as holy, or as symbols of something holy. While we may strive for growth in our spiritual lives, taking an oath can actually be a roadblock if taken too lightly. While swearing on holy symbols may not have the same pomp and circumstance as we find in the formal heathen court, and we may have a lot of pride in our ability to live by the Nine Noble Virtues, is it going to be possible for you to meet the standard of the oath you take when the chips are down? Consider carefully and try harder.

Notes
_____
_____
_____
_____
_____
_____
_____
_____
_____
_____

Religion of the Northmen
Dueling was known among the heathen North men by two names:
hólmgánga and einvígi.

We have spent a great deal of time looking over the idea of justice and to some extent the government of our heathen ancestors; now, lest we forget our roots, we should be reminded that these men had no qualms when it came time to settle a matter the old-fashioned way. Sometimes we are left with the same choice. An unsettled injustice can be like a poison if we let it fester inside and eat away at us. Find a way and get it out; do not be afraid to speak up and out against any injustice someone would do to you.

*Meditate on **Thurisaz** as in Thor a wise warrior.*

Notes
_____
_____
_____
_____
_____
_____
_____
_____
_____
_____

Religion of the Northmen
The Einvígi being the simplest was probably also the oldest form of single combat. It was gradually made more and more complicated, so that the combatants might have better opportunities for displaying their strength and skill.

Given the lack of a battlefield or sometimes even a good backyard, remember that there is always more than one way to skin a cat, or your enemy for that matter. I'm pretty sure it was a smarter opponent who insisted on displays of skill over strength. Be smarter than your opponents.

Notes:

_____

_____

_____

_____

_____

_____

_____

_____

_____

_____

Religion of the Northmen
Although the hólmgang degenerated in this manner into a tool of the basest selfishness, revenge, and wickedness, there is, at the same, time no doubt that it was originally a religious custom, in which the fundamental idea was, that the Gods would make manifest by the issue of the battle which of the contending parties had justice on his side.

This is referring to the troublesome idea of engaging a berserker in hólmgang, and it speaks to us today. Don't be a bully. More importantly, no one is going to treat you as special simply because you tell them you are a heathen.

Meditate on **Hagalaz** *as a rune governing the confrontation of past patterns.*

Notes

_____

_____

_____

_____

_____

_____

_____

_____

_____

_____

Religion of the Northmen
The hólmgang was thus in effect a judgment of the Gods, intimately
connected with the Asa-faith, and among the North men it disappeared
with that faith, at least as a judicial act.

There are many ways we can engage our enemies, but first and foremost
we should be sure we have done the right thing. Selfishness, revenge, and
other short-sighted ego-driven attitudes will get in the way of our spiritual
growth. This seemingly testosterone based idea of single combat for
justice can be the foundation of our own growth. Our toughest opponents
will always be ourselves.

Notes
_____
_____
_____
_____
_____
_____
_____
_____
_____

Prose Edda

Next to these in the figures of poesy are those men who are called chiefs: one may periphrase them as one might a king or an earl, calling them Dispensers of Gold, Wealth Munificent, Men of the Standards, and Captains of the Host, or Van-Leaders of the Array or of Battle; since each king of a nation, who rules over many lands, appoints tributary kings and earls in joint authority with himself, to administer the laws of the land and defend it from attack in those parts which lie far removed from the king. And in those parts they shall be equal with the king's self in giving judgment and meting punishment.

In the end, after careful consideration and a review of the facts, sagas, histories and legends, we find an intelligent and caring people guided by spiritual principles and a solid realization that equality of men and women is best provided for in a society by justice.

Meditate on **Wunjo** *pertaining to the joy and fellowship of like minds.*

Notes

_____

_____

_____

_____

_____

_____

_____

_____

_____

Lenting/March

Courage
_____

Hovamol 16
A cowardly man
thinks he will ever live,
if warfare he avoids;
but old age will
give him no peace,
though spears may spare him.

We see this stanza quite often in Asatru. Sometimes I wonder if it might be the battle cry for the crazy brave and the phony tough. I wish it were not so. It lends itself all too easily to the Viking ideologies that sometimes seem to overwhelm Asatru. But if you can consider the other side of this coin, and see that the daily battles one fights in Valhalla may not be against an opponent but against oneself and the weaknesses that must be conquered, I submit that once your courage has proven sufficient to conquer yourself, your old age will be peaceful indeed.

Meditate on **Ihwaz** *think of Yggdrasil and a vertical axis of becoming who you are supposed to be.*

Notes

_____

_____

_____

_____

_____

_____

_____

_____

_____

_____

Hovamol
(131) I rede thee, Loddfafnir!   And hear thou my rede,-
Profit thou hast if thou hearest,
Great thy gain if thou learnest:
Look not up   when the battle is on,-
(Like madmen the sons   of men become,-)
Lest men bewitch thy wits.

Courage isn't the absence of fear; it's action in the face of it. How
difficult that must be if one were to be faced with everything all at once.
Focus on the task at hand and win one battle at a time.

Notes
_____
_____
_____
_____
_____
_____
_____
_____
_____

Germania
In the day of battle, it is scandalous to the Prince to be surpassed in feats of bravery, scandalous to his followers to fail in matching the bravery of the Prince.

In today's age and given the current stream of thought to which our society subscribes, there is the possibility of a unique interpretation of this statement. This is especially true for the Gothi, Folkbuilder, or Chieftain. Being in a leadership position, I believe it to be essential that we set the standard in everything we can. Whatever we set our minds and hearts to we should finish with gusto, including self-examination. There is no greater proving ground today than to tackle the ego head on and rid yourself of the garbage most people carry around with them. Garbage stinks; get rid of it.

Meditate on **Dagaz** *as in a rune of awakening to your possibilities.*

Notes

_____

_____

_____

_____

_____

_____

_____

_____

_____

_____

Germania
They account fortune amongst things slippery and uncertain, but bravery
amongst such as are never-failing and secure; and, what is exceeding rare
nor ever to be learnt but by a wholesome course of discipline, in the
conduct of the general they repose more assurance than in the strength of
the army.

The actions of the noble minded man or woman, when guided by the
Nine Noble Virtues, can be a beacon to those around, who struggle under
the oppressive yoke of guilt, pain, fear, and suffering. All it takes is the
courage to live a life of worth.

Notes
_____
_____
_____
_____
_____
_____
_____
_____
_____
_____

Germania

But by the Germans the Roman People have been bereft of five armies, all commanded by Consuls; by the Germans, the commanders of these armies, Carbo, and Cassius, and Scaurus Aurelius, and Servilius Caepio, as also Marcus Manlius, were all routed or taken: by the Germans even the Emperor Augustus was bereft of Varus and three legions.

A Roman Army could consist of up to 40,000 men.

Meditate on **Ansuz** *breathe deeply and consider the inspiration of Odin to be a leader.*

Notes

Hovamol 48
The lives of the brave   are noble and best,
    Sorrows they seldom feed;
But the coward fear   of all things feels,
    And not gladly the niggard gives.

Since I've begun the Asatru way of life I am no longer hampered by the thought of "What if I fail?" If we are honest with ourselves, the fear of failure, of not being good enough, stems from a constant barrage of being told to be good or God won't love you and you will end up in hell. At some point we finally become blissfully paralyzed into inactivity, waiting for a kingdom in heaven. This is hogwash, and it is perhaps one of the most liberating ideas I've found in Asatru, that as one of the folk I may walk with my head held high, I have the chance to grow and become all I can be, and I may go anywhere a free man can go. I am not afraid of the "what ifs" anymore.

Notes

Prose Edda
Thor was by no means anxious to avoid the fight when challenged to the field, for no one had ever offered him single-combat before.

The chance to struggle against an opponent and win, the excitement of being challenged, and the anticipation of victory are among those things that make us feel so very alive. We should follow Thor's example and always embrace those personal challenges.

Meditate on **Algiz** *as a connection of yourself and the patterns of the divine*

Notes
_____
_____
_____
_____
_____
_____
_____
_____
_____
_____

Voluspa 52

Now comes Hlin   yet another hurt,
When Othin fares   to fight with the wolf,
And Belis slayer   seeks out Surt,
For there must fall   the joy of Frigg.

Frey fights with the horn of a stag, having given up his legendary sword for love; Odin fights the Fenris wolf though he already knows it will cost him his life. Both Gods fight anyway; in just four short lines they set the example. They are ill prepared to face the oncoming fight for various reasons, but they fight on. Can we do any less in our daily lives? The very few of us who believe vehemently in Asatru have an obligation to live our lives in the face of adversity, and to demonstrate to the world the religion of our ancestors and the positive effects it has had on our lives. The courageous deaths of Odin and Frey pave the way for much better things to come.

*Meditate on **Ehwaz** or teamwork just as Frigga sends Hlin as a protector for Odin, believe in it for yourself as well.*

Notes

_____

_____

_____

_____

_____

_____

_____

_____

_____

Despite decrees by Olaf, Oliver continued to organize and conduct sacrifices and ceremonies celebrating our Gods and Goddesses until an informant led to his capture and execution while preparing for the spring sacrifices.

Oliver sets a fine example for us to follow in the face of difficulty we can only imagine. It's not necessary to lead with the chin, but if we are going to be Asatruar it is up to us to make sure we can point out to naysayers the positive benefits of how our lives are lived today.

Notes

Voluspa 55 - 56

Against the serpent   goes Othins son.

In anger smites   the warder of earth,-
Forth from their homes   must all men flee,-
Nine paces fares   the son of Fjorgyn,
And, slain by the serpent,   fearless he sinks.

The fear of snakes is one of the things that seem to be hardwired into the psyche of mankind. The champion God of earth and mankind goes up against some kind of serpent monster in tale after tale around the world.
With respect to courage, though, Thor demonstrates for us an act of courage second only to Odin's; his mighty struggle and the death of both combatants pave the way for a new earth and a new time of peace for all of us. Perhaps it is just one more way of telling us that before we can become who we are supposed to be and grow as much as we spiritually can, we must fight the greatest monsters within us, even if it seems we may lose something we consider important to us.

Meditate on **Uruz** *the rune of strength and primal power.*

Notes
_____
_____
_____
_____
_____
_____
_____
_____
_____
_____

Skirnismol 13
Skirnir replied:
"Boldness is better   than plaints can be
For him whose feet must fare;
To a destined day   has mine age been doomed,
And my life's span thereto laid."

There is no use to whine about the state of affairs; go forward and do the best you can do. The skein of your life was woven long ago. Be bold and brave and never be afraid to try.

Notes

_____

_____

_____

_____

_____

_____

_____

_____

Skirnismol 24
Gerth spake:
"For no man's sake   will I ever suffer
To be thus moved by might;
But gladly, methinks,   will Gymir seek
To fight if he finds thee here."

A threat from the messenger of Frey would make most folk tremble, but Gerth stands her ground in the face of what is surely impending doom. But on her side is the love of the father who raised her. Many times I've read about, and once or twice put myself in, situations that are terrifying and require a good deal of courage to deal with; in the majority of those crises I've found that courage empowered by love will win the day.

Meditate on **Berkano** *as a rune of growth and new beginnings.*

Notes
_____
_____
_____
_____
_____
_____
_____
_____
_____
_____

Hymiskvitha 13
Eight fell from the ledge,   and one alone,
The hard-hammered kettle,   of all was whole;
Forth came they then,   and his foes he sought,
The giant old,   and held with his eyes.

The introduction of Tyr's father in the Hymikvitha tells of an old, misshapen giant, whose beard is covered in ice. At his glance, mighty beams were broken and seven kettles fell from the ledge and were also broken. But Thor met his gaze. In the face of the cold, dangerous, unforgiving representation of the fiercest elements of nature itself, Thor and Tyr stood side by side with unwavering certainty as to who and what they were. The giants had been waiting on Tyr, though the poem does not say why. Was he expected to come back and bring relief to this giant stock and help them take a step forward? Is Hymer the element that is preventing this, encouraged by his horrible and hated mother? I think this interpretation rings true, and I have to ask myself if there is something in my life that is holding me back. Do I have the courage to stand up to it, knowing there will be a God by my side? Absolutely.

Notes

Lokasenna 42
Loki spake:
"The daughter of Gymir with gold didst thou buy,
And sold thy sword to boot;
But when Muspell's sons through Myrkwood ride,
Thou shalt weaponless wait, poor wretch."

Only a man who lacks inspiration would call this a bad thing. What more powerful story than one of courage emboldened by love. This example of courage enough to live life despite the doom Frey knows he will face is something we would all do well to remember when times become just a little too much. Never quit, and believe in love.

Meditate on **Inguz** *as the seed of the divine within us.*

Notes
_____
_____
_____
_____
_____
_____
_____
_____
_____
_____

Baldrs Draumar 2
Then Othin rose,   the enchanter old,
And the saddle he laid   on Sleipnir's back;
Thence rode he down   to Niflhel deep,
And the hound he met   that came from hell.

Odin's ability to ride the greatest of horses into the very bowels of Niflhel on behalf of his son may not have required quite so much courage from him as it would from me. But when it comes to my children, I find I have no lack of courage, and in truth in today's society, my children are at the top of the list of things in my life well worth fighting for.

Notes

Baldrs Draumar 3
Bloody he was   on his breast before,
At the father of magic   he howled from afar;
Forward rode Othin,   the earth resounded
Till the house so high   of Hel he reached.

Not even the hound of Hel gave Odin pause. He was on an errand on behalf of his son Baldur and he would not be swayed or diverted, nor yield to any challenge. If only today all children could count on the steadfast ability of their parents to raise, protect, and love them.

*Meditate on **Nauthiz** for our children have need of us and we need to be aware of those responsibilities.*

Notes

Hovamol 15
The son of a king   shall be silent and wise,
          And bold in battle as well;
Bravely and gladly   a man shall go,
          Till the day of his death is come.

It takes a lot of work to achieve these attitudes concerning life, whether you are a prince or a pauper. But if you can even begin to achieve this standard, to be silent and wise and bold, to go bravely and gladly forward, what could ever stand in your way?

Notes
_____
_____
_____
_____
_____
_____
_____
_____
_____
_____

Hovamol 64
The man who is prudent   a measured use
Of the might he has will make;
He finds when among the brave he fares
That the boldest he may not be.

We are not all created equal. That's just the way it is. There are men out there who are better than me at a great many things, but if I make good and prudent use of the gifts I have, I will be counted among the wise.

Meditate on **Raidho** *and consider the journey we are all on. What gifts should we use to ensure smooth sailing?*

Notes

_____
_____
_____
_____
_____
_____
_____
_____
_____
_____

Lokasenna 37
Tyr spake:
"Of the heroes brave is Freyr the best
Here in the home of the gods;
He harms not maids nor the wives of men,
And the bound from their fetters he frees."

The last line of the stanza bears the truth about Frey: the bound from their fetters he frees. We often overlook the ability of the Gods to assist us in the really hard times. As a God of prosperity I believe Frey has a vested interest in our success as a demonstration of who he is to us. Today I'm going to believe that.

Notes

_____

_____

_____

_____

_____

_____

_____

_____

_____

Prose Edda
While the Lord of high Bilskirnir,
Whose heart no falsehood fashioned,
Swiftly strove to shatter
The sea-fish with his hammer.

Thor possesses a good and true heart, aside from the many things he owns to make him such a mighty defender of Asgard and protector of mankind. It is his stout and true heart we find referenced first when he strives to smite the Midgard Serpent. The truth is powerful in its own right and we in Asatru should always embrace it.

Meditate on **Sowilo** *as a rune of success.*

Notes

Skirnismol 26
Skirnir spake:
"Seest thou, maiden,   this keen, bright sword
That I hold here in my hand?
Before its blade   the old giant bends,-
Thy father is doomed to die."

The next 13 stanzas of the Skirnismol outline the failings of a life too dearly attached to the world and all its earthly matters to accept the divine intervention of the Gods. At first glance it just appears that the giant maiden is being threatened into accepting the troth of Frey after riches and love fail. These stanzas outline, if we look around us, the sufferings to a greater or lesser degree of the people about us who fail to enlarge upon their spiritual lives. Ugly things begin to eat at their souls, it would seem, and we find them alone and all too often suffering an early or untimely death. We are offered the opportunity to get to know the Aesir on a daily basis, with each new wonderful sunrise. Today I think I will do my best to remain in the sunlight.

Notes
_____
_____
_____
_____
_____
_____
_____
_____
_____
_____

Lokasenna 4
Eldir spake;
"If in thou goest to Ægir's hall,
And fain the feast wouldst see,
And with slander and spite wouldst sprinkle the gods,
Think well lest they wipe it on thee."

People who sling mud usually get a lot of it on them.

Meditate on **Gebo** *and remember generosity and hospitality.*

Notes
_____
_____
_____
_____
_____
_____
_____
_____
_____
_____

Prose Edda

And at evening, when it was time for drinking, Odin had swords brought
into the hall, so bright that light radiated from them: and other
illumination was not used while they sat at drinking. Then the Æsir came
in to their banquet, and in the high-seats sat them down those twelve Æsir
who were appointed to be judges; these were their names: Thor, Njördr,
Freyr, Týr, Heimdallr, Bragi, Vídarr, Váli, Ullr, Hœnir, Forseti, Loki; and
in like manner the Asynjur: Frigg, Freyja, Gefjun, Idunn, Gerdr, Sigyn,
Fulla, Nanna. It seemed glorious to Ægir to look about him in the hall: the
wain-scottings there were all hung with fair shields; there was also
stinging mead, copiously quaffed.

A fantastic description of the community of our Gods and Goddesses.
Could we ever be so blessed as to encounter such a setting? While I do
not subscribe much to role playing and re-enactment, I wonder what we
could achieve if our ceremonies could be held with the same feeling I
enjoy reading just this paragraph. A flood of sincerity and community,
knowing the individual next to you is enjoying their relation with the
divine as much as you are.

Notes
_____
_____
_____
_____
_____
_____
_____
_____
_____
_____

Voluspa 24

Then sought the gods   their assembly-seats,
    The holy ones,   and council held,
    Whether the gods   should tribute give,
Or to all alike   should worship belong.

The Gods of the Sky and of the Earth give us an example concerning equality. Each God is secure in who and what he/she is. Out of that confidence in their own heritage we may take the suggestion that we also have a mighty heritage to lay claim to, though it does not make us more or less important than the other races. Once our own confidence is firmly in place, we can deal with others from a position of security and our decisions no longer need to be based upon fear or hate.

Meditate on **Laguz** *like the oceans and the wells it is our collective memory.*

Notes
_____
_____
_____
_____
_____
_____
_____
_____
_____
_____

Prose Edda

XXXI. "How should man be paraphrased? By his works, by that which he gives or receives or does; he may also be paraphrased in terms of his property, those things which he possesses, and, if he be liberal, of his liberality;......likewise in terms of the families from which he descended, as well as of those which have sprung from him."

Not once does this say a man should be paraphrased by what he says. Deeds not words.

Notes

Hovamol 32
Friendly of mind   are many men,
Till feasting they mock at their friends;
To mankind a bane   must it ever be
When guests together strive.

The bane of mankind, to sit around and engage in character assassination in an attempt to make ourselves appear more than we really are. No tribe, kindred, or community can survive long with this type of selfish behavior.

Meditate on **Thurisaz** *and the defense Thor provides the men of midgard*

Notes

Hovamol 62
When the eagle comes   to the ancient sea,
He snaps and hangs his head;
So is a man   in the midst of a throng,
Who few to speak for him finds.

Many times I've felt alone in a crowd and it hurts. In our Asatru community we have groups of friends, but all of us have a new-found view of the world in which we live, and the eagerness we have to share that creates an atmosphere I have found comfortable and accepting.

Notes
_____
_____
_____
_____
_____
_____
_____
_____
_____

Hovamol 69
All wretched is no man,   though never so sick;
    Some from their sons have joy,
Some win it from kinsmen,   and some from their wealth,
    And some from worthy works.

All of us have a role to play in the building of this worthy way of life we call Asatru. Not everyone will become a Gothi, or a senator, or maybe not even a foreman at the job they work. This passage assures us there is more than one way to skin a cat as the old saying goes. Do your best at whatever you do.

Meditate on **Jera** *a harvest of right action*

Notes
_____
_____
_____
_____
_____
_____
_____
_____
_____

Hovamol 134
I rede thee, Loddfafnir!   And hear thou my rede,-
Profit thou hast if thou hearest,
Great thy gain if thou learnest:
Scorn or mocking   ne'er shalt thou make
Of a guest or a journey-goer.

It's always our ego talking whenever we make an assumption about a
stranger. To put it into words or act upon it simply because we may think
we are better than they are is the root of folly. In old times the stories
were told of Gods and Goddesses visiting this realm on overcast days, as
they would cast no shadow. Even if we never witness something like
that, to be able to engage another in a manner that makes that person's life
a little better – even if it's just a smile – quite clearly makes for a life
worth living.

Notes

Hovamol 158
An eleventh I know,   if needs I must lead
To the fight my long-loved friends;
I sing in the shields,   and in strength they go
Whole to the field of fight,
Whole from the field of fight,
And whole they come thence home.

Even though a warrior's death is a guarantee to Valhalla or Folksvang.
Asatru serves life and we are not meant to be spending our days preparing
for life in heaven by doing nothing. The community needs its protectors
and fathers and sons and that means our focus should be on the here and
now. The eleventh spell is to ensure that the leader of men can bring his
men home, with victory and life. To lead men and secure their safety,
I've got to be as prepared as possible and as developed as possible; the lives
of a great many people will be affected if I don't get it right. I have to ask
myself if I have done my best to develop myself to handle the leadership
challenge.

Meditate on **Raidho** *the journey is the destination*

Notes

Skirnismol 6-8
Freyr spake:
"From Gymir's house   I beheld go forth
A maiden dear to me;
Her arms glittered,   and from their gleam
Shown all the sea and sky.

"To me more dear   than in days of old
Was ever maiden to man;
But no one of gods   or elves will grant
That we both together should be."

Ed em
("Hither to me   shalt thou bring the maid,
And home shalt thou lead her here,
If her father wills it   or wills it not,
And good reward shalt thou get.")

These three stanzas may appear to be relatively straightforward and yet they really aren't. Throughout religious literature and myth we have example after example of the divine and holy expressing a desire to interact with the folk that worship and hold them in such high esteem. Skirnir is offered the chance to be a divine messenger on behalf of Frey and is promised great reward in return. Is it possible to fashion ourselves a life based on principle, that as closely as possible aligns itself with what we hold divine, and to receive our own great reward? Perhaps we should try.

*Meditate on **Sowilo** the sun as a rune of success*

Notes
_____
_____
_____
_____
_____
_____
_____
_____
_____
_____
_____

Ostara/April

Generosity

Hyndlujoth 3
"Triumph to some, and treasure to others,
To many wisdom and skill in words,
Fair winds to the sailor, to the singer his art,
And a manly heart to many a hero."

This speaks of Odin's gifts to the heroes, warriors, and kings of the sagas.
His generosity to his favorites is legendary throughout the sagas and
Eddas. Odin's gifts are not limited to just one aspect of a person's being;
this is one of the reasons he is referred to as the Allfather. As parents we
are obligated to ensure our future generations are also well rounded
individuals and capable of carrying this faith well into the future.

*Meditate on **Othala** to manifest our own divine inheritance.*

Notes

_____

_____

_____

_____

_____

_____

_____

_____

_____

_____

Hovamol 148
The songs I know   that king's wives know not,
Nor men that are sons of men;
The first is called help,   and help it can bring thee
In sorrow and pain and sickness.

The first song is a song of help. An offer of assistance in a time of need. A reminder for those who study these ancient texts that our Gods are here to help those who have taken the time to delve deeper into their mysteries. In doing so and incorporating those lessons as deeply into our being as we are capable of, we may find ourselves in touch with that spark of the divine within us. This allows us to help ourselves thru many a tough time. Quite a blessing indeed.

Notes
_____
_____
_____
_____
_____
_____
_____
_____
_____

Germania
Upon your departure, if you ask anything, it is the custom to grant it; and with the same facility, they ask of you.

This is an ideal that is anathema to today's standards, our selfish lifestyles, and obsession with "keeping up with the Joneses," which had no place in our ancestors' lives. And far from being a frivolous idea, it is firmly rooted in the idea that this individual is worth far more than some possession.

Notes

_____

_____

_____

_____

_____

_____

_____

_____

_____

_____

Germania
In gifts they delight, but neither claim merit from what they give, nor own any obligation for what they receive.

The very root of the sentiment that it is better to give than to receive. Nothing creates a more brilliant smile on a friend's face than to give.

*Meditate on **Gebo** as the runic symbol for gift.*

Notes

_____

_____

_____

_____

_____

_____

_____

_____

_____

_____

Hovamol 40
None so free with gifts   or food have I found
That gladly he took not a gift;
Nor one who so widely   scattered his wealth
That of recompense hatred he had.

The wealthy have the opportunity to seemingly change the world; with gifts and praise they draw many to their cause and garner the support of most of the people to whom they have shown kindness. But sometimes those that gift all the time need that little pat on the back, and it may come from the simplest of tokens when presented from the heart. Amazingly, that simple action could bring about mighty changes in itself.

Notes

Hovamol 41
Friends shall gladden each other with arms and garments,
As each for himself can see;
Gift-givers' friendships   are longest found,
If fair their fates may be.

The idea of gift exchange can be found in almost every religion. The giving of a gift has a remarkable capacity to beat down the walls of importance and ego, to level the playing field among men and women, and to make a lasting friendship that can withstand something more than just the easy times.

Meditate on **Wunjo** *and the happiness generosity can produce*

Notes
_____
_____
_____
_____
_____
_____
_____
_____
_____

Hovamol 42
To his friend a man   a friend shall prove,
    And gifts with gifts requite;
But men shall mocking   with mockery answer,
    And fraud with falsehood meet.

To make a friend, be a friend; and when the situation is favorable, a simple exchange of gifts is most appropriate. But by the same token, while we wholeheartedly offer friendship to those who deserve it, there should be no hesitation in dealing equally as forcefully with those who would seek to bring us down.

Notes

_____

_____

_____

_____

_____

_____

_____

_____

_____

Hovamol 52
No great thing needs   a man to give,
        Oft little will purchase praise;
    With half a loaf   and a half-filled cup
        A friend full fast I made.

It's not always the grand gestures of goodwill and gift giving that promote Asatru the best. Once we have made this faith a way of life, the simple actions of kindness may go the furthest.

*Meditate on **Gebo** the gift*

Notes
_____
_____
_____
_____
_____
_____
_____
_____
_____

On this day of remembrance to Jarl Haakon take a little while and think about how your actions help or hinder the advancement of our Faith among the folk and back into mainstream society.

Now do it.

Notes

_____

_____

_____

_____

_____

_____

_____

_____

_____

_____

Hyndlujoth 2
"The favours of Heerfather seekwe to find,
To his followers' gold he gladly gives;
To Hermoth gave he helm and mail-coat,
And to Sigmund he gave a sword as gift."

Specific examples of the gifts and the generosity of Odin, given to heroes who accomplished great deeds that we read about even today. Why would we ever have to doubt that a God with so many names – each one indicating an attribute of his greatness – would not gift us as well? We each have something special within us worth sharing. The challenge is to figure out which dragon to slay to allow that gift to develop.

Mediatate on **Dagaz** *, a rune of awakening.*

Notes
_____
_____
_____
_____
_____
_____
_____
_____
_____

Grimnismol 2
'Twixt the fires now   eight nights have I sat,
And no man brought meat to me,
Save Agnar alone and alone shall rule
Geirröth's son o'er the Goths.

With a simple act of kindness, he has done the right thing, and he is rewarded with his own kingdom. In our lives each day we have control of how we are perceived in our own little kingdom, our circle of friends. Once you begin acting generously with others, see how rich your world can become, if nothing more than in the esteem in which your friends hold you.

Notes

_____

_____

_____

_____

_____

_____

_____

_____

Grimnismol 3
Hail to thee, Agnar!   For hailed thou art
By the voice of Veratyr;
For a single drink   shalt thou never receive
A greater gift as reward.

In the Grimnismal, we see Odin offering a clear and precise description of Asgard. At first glance it seems to be a retelling of material in the Voluspa and other poems. But if we pay attention we see that Odin, or Veratyr (God that is), is giving to Agnar much more than just a kingdom; he is in fact explaining to him the secrets of the universe. Everything he tells him has some kind of esoteric meaning if we have the mind to perceive it. That is indeed a mighty gift: to be handed knowledge and wisdom from Odin as a reward for a simple kindness.

*Meditate on **Inguz** the seed of the divine within us.*

Notes

Prose Edda
For that Grjótbjörn
In goods and gear
Freyr and Njördr
Have fairly blessed.

This is the type of generosity I think we could all handle – receiving blessings from the Gods that govern treasure, prosperity, the sea, and Alfland. A favorable nod from the two of them – it is possible, it is something we can believe in. The requirement to be generous with each other is not limited to the interactions between men, but extends to the Gods' interactions with us and vice versa.

Notes

_____

_____

_____

_____

_____

_____

_____

_____

_____

Prose Edda
Ívaldi's offspring
In ancient days
Went to shape Skídbladnir,
Foremost of ships,
Fairly for Freyr,
Choicely for Njördr's child.

That a God of prosperity and fertility, Frey – himself a gift to humanity from the God of the seas, the wind, and treasures untold, Njord – would be given a craft to navigate the patterns of the seas his father rules is significant. It is an example of what we can expect from the Allfather: he has gifted us the Eddas and the runes, in the hope that we may also successfully navigate the seas of life and enjoy all the rewards this life has to offer.

Meditate on **Jera** *a harvest of right action.*

Notes

_____

Voluspa 4
Then Burs sons lifted   the level land;
Mithgarth the mighty   there they made;
The sun from the south   warmed the stones of the earth,
And green was the ground   with growing leeks.

Once Odin had ascended to the point at which he had created a world of order out of the chaos of the primal forces, he continued to grow and develop, partly through the exercise of generosity to the world of men.
Once we have raised ourselves to a level at which we can accept the radiance of divinity, we will also begin to experience the abundance that is symbolized by the leek.

Notes

_____

_____

_____

_____

_____

_____

_____

_____

_____

_____

Prose Edda

XXXI. "How should man be paraphrased? By his works, by that which he gives or receives or does; be may also be paraphrased in terms of his property, those things which he possesses, and, if he be liberal, of his liberality."

One of the measures of a man is his generosity.

Meditate on **Wunjo** *and the joy of a fellowship of like minds.*

Notes

_____

_____

_____

_____

_____

_____

_____

_____

_____

Voluspa 17-18

Then from the throng	did three come forth,
From the home of the gods,	the mighty and gracious;
Two without fate	on the land they found,
Ask and Embla,	empty of might.
Soul they had not,	sense they had not,
Heat nor motion,	nor goodly hue;
Soul gave Othin,	sense gave Honir,
Heat gave Lothur	and goodly hue.

These gifts from Odin and his brothers enable to us to ascend in our own right, and under the right circumstances to aid the Gods in their mission. This is a gift that keeps on giving, and that gives usa chance to become a force that Odin himself would take note of and wish to have on his side.

Notes

_____

_____

_____

_____

_____

_____

_____

_____

_____

_____

Hovamol 142
Nine mighty songs   I got from the son
Of Bolthorn, Bestla's father;
And a drink I got   of the goodly mead
Poured out from Othrörir.

Once Odin had made his sacrifice and symbolically removed that which was interfering with his true vision, then his family began to share with him. Who can help but to wonder what those nine mighty songs could be. Once we begin to make sacrifices for the sake of growth we can also expect generosity from life itself to better our own lives.

Meditate on **Alghiz** *and your connection with the patterns of the divine.*

Notes

_____

_____

_____

_____

_____

_____

_____

_____

_____

Hovamol 144
Runes shalt thou find,   and fateful signs,
That the king of singers colored,
And the mighty gods have made;
Full strong the signs,   full mighty the signs
That the ruler of gods doth write.

This gift of the runes, these keys to the universe itself, should be counted among our best gifts. When we get it in perspective our Gods have been generous with us indeed.

Notes
_____
_____
_____
_____
_____
_____
_____
_____
_____
_____

Hovamol 166
Long these songs   thou shalt, Loddfafnir,
Seek in vain to sing;
Yet good it were   if thou mightest get them,
Well, if thou wouldst them learn,
Help, if thou hadst them.

Just as with many sage teachings, we are given notice that these songs exist and that within them, as within the runes, there are answers. But not for the uninitiated. Those who devote themselves to learning, living, and applying the Nine Noble Virtues in their daily lives will come to understand the truth of these sayings and songs as they grow in spirit.

Meditate on **Ihwaz** *as the Yew or Yggdrasil and envision ascending its trunk.*

Notes

_____

_____

_____

_____

_____

_____

_____

_____

_____

Hovamol 132
I rede thee, Loddfafnir!   And hear thou my rede,-
Profit thou hast if thou hearest,
Great thy gain if thou learnest:
If thou fain wouldst win   a woman's love,
And gladness get from her,
Fair be thy promise   and well fulfilled;
None loathes what good he gets.

An honest and simple expression of love and the continued mighty effort to deliver on those words from the heart will deliver good to your life everyday.

Notes

_____

_____

_____

_____

_____

_____

_____

_____

_____

_____

Hovamol 139

I rede thee, Loddfafnir!   and hear thou my rede,-
Profit thou hast if thou hearest,
Great thy gain if thou learnest:
When ale thou drinkest,   seek might of earth,
(For earth cures drink,   and fire cures ills,
The oak cures tightness,   the ear cures magic,
Rye cures rupture,   the moon cures rage,
Grass cures the scab,   and runes the sword-cut;)
The field absorbs the flood.
Now are Hor's words   spoken in the hall,
Kind for the kindred of men,
Cursed for the kindred of giants:
Hail to the speaker,   and to him who learns!
Profit be his who has them!
Hail to them who hearken!

We are told at the beginning of the stanza and at the end of it that this stuff is worth knowing. There is great value in taking the time to consider what has been said. I would wager that if we were to take the time and look at these statements beyond what is obvious on the surface of them and the old wives' tales that are associated with them, true science that would support these ideas and amaze us.

Meditate on **Kenaz** *the torch of knowledge.*

Notes
_____
_____
_____
_____
_____
_____
_____
_____
_____
_____

Hovamol 146

Knowest how one shall write,	knowest how one shall rede?
Knowest how one shall tint,	knowesthow one makes trial?
Knowest how one shall ask,	knowesthow one shall offer?
Knowest how one shall send,	knowesthow one shall sacrifice?

In these rhetorical questions, we can almost sense a challenge. For the most part the counsel given to Loddfafner is straightforward and easy to understand. But as we progress further into the Havamal and the 18 songs or spells which Odin knows and explains to us, we find ourselves at a loss. If we decide to, we may use it as a catapult to launch us into further learning that will more closely align our souls, if you will, with the purposes of the Gods. Only after we have grown sufficiently spiritually will we be able to utilize what to all intents and purposes appears to be a font of power unlike most to which we are accustomed. There is the possibility that we may not understand them until after our physical forms die. We have to consider that the truth upon which we gaze is as incomprehensible to us as mathematics to a beetle. Now how shall we rectify that situation today?

Notes

_____

_____

_____

_____

_____

_____

_____

_____

_____

_____

Skirnismol 15
Gerth spake:
"What noise is that   which now so loud
I hear within our house?
The ground shakes,   and the home of Gymir
Around me trembles too."

What an interesting statement made by someone who is about to be visited by an avatar of the divine. As I reflect upon my entry in Asatru it may not have been as dramatic, but I assure you it has been a 180-degree turn in my perception of the world, my place in it, and my relation with the Aesir. That change in perception is still happening. But now it requires a little more knowledge, as was the case for Gerd, to understand what is happening and how it is going to better me.

Meditate on **Hagalaz***, hail and radical change.*

Notes
_____
_____
_____
_____
_____
_____
_____
_____
_____
_____

Voluspa 53

Then comes Sigfather's	mighty son,
Vithar, to fight	with the foaming wolf;
In the giant's son	does he thrust his sword
Full to the heart:	his father is avenged.

At first glance we see the loyal and loving son killing the monster which took his father's life. But if we take into account the whole of the story – including Ragnarok and the end of the Gods and subsequent rebirth of the Aesir, minus their imperfections – it can be argued in an esoteric manner that this is an example of the son not falling victim to the evils that plagued the father. When the son does emerge victorious, it ushers in a new era of prosperity for the next generation of Gods and men under Baldur's guidance. The shining son has been reborn to oversee nine realms of his own. The cycle of growth begins anew.

Notes

_____

_____

_____

_____

_____

_____

_____

_____

_____

_____

_____

Hovamol 72
A son is better,   though late he be born,
   And his father to death have fared;
Memory-stones   seldom stand by the road
   Save when kinsman honours his kin.

The greatest gift we leave the world and the measure by which we shall be judged by others is the quality of people our children become.

Meditate on **Laguz** *the ocean of our collective memory.*

Notes
_____
_____
_____
_____
_____
_____
_____
_____
_____
_____

Hovamol 47
Young was I once,   and wandered alone,
     And naught of the road I knew;
Rich did I feel   when a comrade I found,
     For man is man's delight.

There is a lot of promise in this stanza. A friendship made on the long
and wandering road of life, about which each of us knows just a little, can
be such a rewarding experience in those times when we get a little lost.
Fellowship of one sort or another has helped many a man come back to
reality. Imagine if the relationship is watered with a little loyalty how
long it can last. Indeed it is a staple in the nutrition of a healthy marriage.

Notes

_____
_____
_____
_____
_____
_____
_____
_____
_____

Skirnismol 23
Gerth spake:
"The ring I wish not,   though burned it was
Of old with Othin's son;
In Gymir's home   is no lack of gold
In the wealth my father wields."

A gift of almost untold of wealth is offered, and still she denies it because of who she believes herself to be. She will not yield her principles though clearly to the outsider looking in it would be the wise choice. Make sure when you engage this attitude that it does not rely on the wealth of someone or some organization not in your control. Make your decisions based upon what you can do for yourself.

Meditate on **Perthro**, *the lot cup and luck.*

Notes

_____

_____

_____

_____

_____

_____

_____

_____

_____

_____

Hovamol 141
None made me happy   with loaf or horn,
          And there below I looked;
I took up the runes,   shrieking I took them,
          And forthwith back I fell.

Odin tells here what it took to gain one of the greatest gifts we have received from him. There was no help from anyone, but he didn't need it. When accepting a gift I try to bear in mind what it took to procure that item.

Notes

_____

_____

_____

_____

_____

_____

_____

_____

_____

_____

Skirnismol 21
Gerth spake:
"I will not take   at any man's wish
These eleven apples ever;
Nor shall Freyr and I   one dwelling find
So long as we two live."

Here we have the offer of a gift of near immortality from Frey himself, yet Gerth shuns it based upon the principles of who she believes herself to be. Her steadfast belief in her place in the world around her can be admired on the one hand, and yet we should be aware that it is also preventing her from achieving a certain form of enlightenment. We should always try to be aware if our sights are set on goals that are good for us.

Meditate on **Uruz** *for strength.*

Notes

Merrymoon/May

Hospitality

Hovamol 2
Givers, hail!
A guest is come in:
where shall he sit?
In much haste is he,
who on the ways has
to try his luck.

In this one stanza we are introduced to hospitality and generosity; we are also reminded to be mindful of the condition of others. What challenges has life thrown at them and how can we help them?

*Meditate on **Nauthiz** concerning necessity.*

Notes

Hovamol 3
Fire is needful
to him who is come in,
and whose knees are frozen;
food and raiment
a man requires,
who o'er the fell has travelled.

This is such a simple idea. I wonder why it is we should need to be made aware of such a common courtesy. Perhaps I should stop and make sure I am not so wrapped up in myself that I neglect the basics for those around me.

Notes

_____

_____

_____

_____

_____

_____

_____

_____

_____

Hovamol 4
Water to him is needful
who for refection comes,
a towel and hospitable invitation,
a good reception;
if he can get it,
discourse and answer.

These basics that we should offer the traveler come with a requirement.
In this passage there is a suggestion we should do it with a "good
reception" – a welcome hello as it were. It's difficult to extend the
courtesy of polite conversation when you feel you are being taken
advantage of. There is no promise of a reward. It takes a well rounded,
mentally and emotionally developed individual to offer what he has to a
stranger. The ability to do it without feeling you are being imposed upon
requires growth. Can you see past your limitations to do this?

*Meditate on **Raidho** our journey.*

Notes
_____
_____
_____
_____
_____
_____
_____
_____
_____
_____

Hovamol 4 (Cottle)
A Drink needeth   to full dishes who cometh, a towel and the prayer to
partake; good bearing eke,   to be well liked and be bidden to banquet
again.

This is the same idea but with a slightly different bent to it. We are
reminded as both travelers and hosts that each has a responsibility to
respect the needs of the other.

Notes
_____
_____
_____
_____
_____
_____
_____
_____
_____

Rigsthula 4
A loaf of bread   did Edda bring,
Heavy and thick   and swollen with husks;
Forth on the table   she sat the fare,
And broth for the meal   in a bowl there was.
(Calf's flesh boiled   was the best of dainties.)

When Rig entered this home they had no idea that he was a God with their and mankind's best interests at heart. They served up the very best for the stranger, and he in return left them with a blessing as well. In today's society if we were to serve up our very best in the things we do, how much of a difference would that make for us all?

Meditate on **Fehu***, wealth.*

Notes

Rigsthula 31

Then forth she brought   the vessels full,
With silver covered,   and set before them,
Meat all browned,   and well-cooked birds;
In the pitcher was wine,   of plate were the cups,
So drank they and talked   till the day was gone.

This cardinal virtue – hospitality – of Germanic antiquity has no boundaries when it comes to societal standing. The best is offered and the company is enjoyed. We do our best to recreate this atmosphere at our events and most times we succeed; as our movement grows we will be given the chance to enjoy this fellowship more and more. It is a goal well worth working towards.

Notes

_____

_____

_____

_____

_____

_____

_____

_____

_____

Germania
Every man receives every comer, and treats him with repasts as large as
his ability can possibly furnish.

The more we ponder this the more we begin to realize that only someone
who is comfortable with who he is, and is secure in the knowledge that he
lives in a community of like-minded, confident individuals, can extend
hospitality in this manner. If we think about this for a moment it
becomes apparent that a society based upon these principles is one well
worth emulating and sharing with those folk around us.

Meditate on **Wunjo**, *joy and fellowship.*

Notes

_____

_____

_____

_____

_____

_____

_____

_____

_____

_____

Skirnismol 17
Gerth spake:
"Bid the man come in,   and drink good mead
Here within our hall;
Though this I fear,   that there without
My brother's slayer stands."

Taken at face value this is a difficult stanza to understand; we are told later on in the Havamal not to trust a brother's killer, and yet here a jotun recognizes her brother's slayer and still invites him in. In another story, a female jotun assists Tyr and Thor in gaining a container large enough to brew mead for Aegir's hall. It has been suggested that the race of giants represents the most base sort of men, specifically those without any enlightenment or spiritual development. These jotuns may well be examples of growth. Gerth's understanding that she needs development and interaction with the Gods begins with letting a representative of the Gods in the door.

Notes

_____

_____

_____

_____

_____

_____

_____

_____

_____

_____

Today we take the time to celebrate a king who would not relinquish his ancestral heritage and his right to pray as he pleased. He spoke out against the forced conversions to Christianity taking place in Norway, and Olaf had his tongue removed because of it.

Do not back down when someone questions or tries to diminish your beliefs. Stand up for the organization you are a part of.

*Meditate on **Ehwaz** for teamwork and trust.*

Notes

_____

_____

_____

_____

_____

_____

_____

_____

_____

_____

Germania
A society, in which every individual, from birth to death, was bound by consideration for his neighbor.

This is a reference to the Germanic peoples as a whole. If we could possibly begin to implement this as sincerely as our ancestors did, the distances we have to travel to enjoy each other's company wouldn't seem nearly as far.

Notes

_____

_____

_____

_____

_____

_____

_____

_____

_____

_____

Lokasenna 10
Othin spake:
"Stand forth then, Vithar, and let the wolf's father
Find a seat at our feast;
Lest evil should Loki speak aloud
Here within Ægir's hall."

Even though all present know Loki is up to no good, the Allfather himself stands fast in the obligation to offer hospitality. It is quite likely Odin knows what Loki is about to do, and the last two lines could be interpreted as a threat or at the least a chance for Loki not to go through with what will become his own undoing. Do we strive as a people to develop such a connection with our spiritual path of Asatru? Can we become aware of these situations and avoid them?

Meditate on **Berkano,** *the birch goddess of renewal.*

Notes
_____
_____
_____
_____
_____
_____
_____
_____
_____

Germania
In social feasts, and deeds of hospitality, no nation upon earth was ever more liberal and abounding.

Only a people confident in who they are and their relation with their Gods can behave in such a manner. Am I capable of developing such a relation with my Gods and myself?

Notes

_____

_____

_____

_____

_____

_____

_____

_____

_____

Germania
To refuse admitting under your roof any man whatsoever, is held wicked and inhuman.

In an age of no trespassing and no soliciting signs and any of a host of other rules required of a person to be admitted conditionally onto your property, this must seem an impossible virtue to live up to and quite possibly a dangerous one. It has been submitted that just such an attitude was one taken advantage of by missionaries to eradicate our beliefs. Yet here we are a millennium later. Today our challenge is how best to apply it; the choice is ours, but hospitality goes a long way to making the folk who and what we are supposed to become.

Meditate on **Ehwaz***, teamwork and trust.*

Notes
_____
_____
_____
_____
_____
_____
_____
_____
_____
_____

Germania
When the whole stock is consumed, he who had treated so hospitably guides and accompanies his guest to a new scene of hospitality; and both proceed to the next house, though neither of them invited. Nor avails it, that they were not: they are there received, with the same frankness and humanity.

Every Asatruevent I have attended has seemed to have such an atmosphere. Each heathen home I have been invited to has held to this grand idea. When I think about it, the concept has connotations of an almost utopian society. I notice the last word chosen for this paragraph is "humanity" – what a clever choice, for in this hospitality to our guest we may well find the seeds of our own freedom.

Notes
_____
_____
_____
_____
_____
_____
_____
_____
_____
_____

Germania
Between a stranger and an acquaintance, in dispensing the rules and
benefits of hospitality, no difference is made.

Service work for a national organization affords me the chance to put this
into practice. Some days it's a piece of cake; some days require that I grow
just a little in an effort to make a new friend and share just a little of what
Asatru is doing in my life, and hopefully theirs as well.

Meditate on **Jera** *a harvest of right action.*

Notes

_____

_____

_____

_____

_____

_____

_____

_____

_____

Germania
Their manner of entertaining their guests is familiar and kind.

A goal we should all strive to meet. Not entertaining in the vapid self-important style we see all too often on reality TV, but with heartfelt desire to provide a lasting impression upon those who share our faith. These kinds of things people will remember. These kinds of simple actions are mentioned time and again in the Eddas and sagas. The manner in which a guest has been treated is usually mentioned and lays the groundwork for the rest of the story. It will make a difference in the rest of your story as well.

Notes
_____
_____
_____
_____
_____
_____
_____
_____
_____
_____

Hovamol 137
I rede thee, Loddfafnir!   And hear thou my rede,-
Profit thou hast if thou hearest,
Great thy gain if thou learnest:
Curse not thy guest,   nor show him thy gate,
Deal well with a man in want.

Profit if you hear and great gain if you learn. All of the aforementioned phrases about hospitality for this month could very well be taken from this stanza. The ability to live by this stanza when it comes to hospitality has many rewards, not the least of which are renown among the folk, and the opportunity to build new friendships as well as to grow spiritually in dealing with the man in want. His actions could be awkward in a social setting but the realization of his condition and a different approach to it could make such a difference in both of your lives.

Meditate on **Gebo** *a gift.*

Notes

_____
_____
_____
_____
_____
_____
_____
_____
_____

Hovamol 138
Strong is the beam   that raised must be
To give an entrance to all;
Give it a ring,   or grim will be
The wish it would work on thee.

The second half of this stanza confirms the idea that it takes a secure, confident individual to "give entrance to all." Like it says, the beam must be raised. The last two lines I suspect mean that if you wish to be entertained in a suitable manner when traveling you should do so at home.

Notes

_____

_____

_____

_____

_____

_____

_____

_____

_____

Prose Edda
A guest shall leave betimes and not stay too long;
Pleasure palls if he lingers too long at another's board.

It's just that simple: don't overstay your welcome. Don't do something that would make a person regret doing their best to follow their faith.

Meditate on **Tiwaz** *as a rune of honor.*

Notes

_____

_____

_____

_____

_____

_____

_____

_____

_____

Grimnismol

In the darkness of the night they were wrecked on the shore; and going up, they found a poor peasant, with whom they stayed through the winter. The housewife took care of Agnar, and the peasant cared for Geirröth, and taught him wisdom.

The unfailing hospitality of the Germanic peoples is seen at work here, while the failing of a man to follow suit as he was taught has dire consequences in this story of Agnar and Geirröth. Now I do not suppose in this day and age we would have to physically suffer in the same manner as Geirröth does later in this story, but words and actions of rudeness directed towards a guest can lead to such a diverse and wide array of societal backlash among the folk, perhaps we should best avoid it. This requires us to be better people. What's the best way I can improve myself to make this a little easier and live up to a standard set forth by the Gods?

Notes

_____

_____

_____

_____

_____

_____

_____

_____

_____

_____

Egil's Saga
Never had he fewer freedmen about his home than a hundred; he was
open-handed and liberal, and readily made friends with the great, and
with all that were near him. A mighty man he became, and he bestowed
much care on his ships, equipment, and weapons.

Following the instructions of the Eddas with respect to his guests and the
men around him, Thorolf prospered and became a great man. He helped
to ensure the success of others and it paid off handsomely. He seems
brave and generous and hospitable. His courage allowed him to enact
these ideals in his life. This is living the Nine Noble Virtues.

Meditate on **Ansuz** *Woden himself.*

Notes
_____
_____
_____
_____
_____
_____
_____
_____
_____
_____

Vafthruthnismol 8-9
Othin spake:
"Gagnrath they call me,   and thirsty I come
From a journey hard to thy hall;
Welcome I look for,   for long have I fared,
And gentle greeting, giant."

Vafthruthnir spake:
"Why standest thou here   on the floor whilst thou speakest?
A seat shalt thou have in my hall;
Then soon shall we know   whose knowledge is more,
The guest's or the sage's gray."

A straight reminder of the requirements of hospitality. The host recognizes that this persona understands the implied intricacies of hospitality and has the confidence of self to apply them freely, even though they each understand this is a test – one that will take a life. Do we each have that kind of courage?

Notes

_____

_____

_____

_____

_____

_____

_____

_____

_____

Gripisspo 7
From the hall the ruler   of heroes went,
And greeted well   the warrior come:
"Sigurth, welcome   long since had been thine;
Now, Geitir, shalt thou   Grani take."

As the ruler (Gripir) is introduced, we see he is a ruler of heroes and we hold him in high regard to begin with. His warm greeting to the warrior raises our esteem of him even more. This demonstrates for us how important hospitality truly is. It is the first impression we give of ourselves.

Meditate on *Wunjo* as a joyful person makes a fine, first impression.

Notes
_____
_____
_____
_____
_____
_____
_____
_____
_____
_____

Gripisspo 8
Then of many   Things they talked,
When thus the men   so wise had met.

This little stanza is beautiful to me as it very simply illustrates, after the warm welcome, confident and wise men enjoying a fine conversation.

Notes
_____
_____
_____
_____
_____
_____
_____
_____
_____
_____

Hymiskvitha 15
Much sorrow his heart   foretold when he saw
The giantess' foeman   come forth on the floor;
Then of the steers   did they bring in three;
Their flesh to boil   did the giant bid.

Even in the face of what most certainly will be disastrous change, because the jotun knows no other way to change, the giant still bears his responsibility well and feeds his son and Thor with a mighty feast of three oxen. Maybe when we notice such change appearing in our own lives we should also embrace it for better or worse. Change is neither good nor bad; our reaction to it is what makes the difference.

Meditate on *Hagalaz* and confronting past patterns to effect change

Notes
_____
_____
_____
_____
_____
_____
_____
_____
_____

Lokasenna 8
Bragi spake:
"A place and a seat will the gods prepare
No more in their midst for thee;
For the gods know well what men they wish
To find at their mighty feasts."

The honor of hospitality is such that we do not have to let miscreants sit with us, according to Bragi. If you find yourself in such a situation, before you fly off the handle, ask what you have done to put yourself in this situation.   Folk in good standing who live by the Nine Noble Virtues are fully aware, or should be, of whether they are measuring up to be counted among the folk. These folk will always be greeted with a smile and a warm welcome.

Notes

_____

_____

_____

_____

_____

_____

_____

_____

_____

_____

Hovamol 136
I rede thee, Loddfafnir!   and hear thou my rede,-
Profit thou hast if thou hearest,
Great thy gain if thou learnest:
Scorn not ever   the grey-haired singer,
Oft do the old speak good;
(Oft from shriveled skin   come skillful counsels,
Though it hang with the hides,
And flap with the pelts,
And is blown with the bellies.)

As we age and lose the bronze glow of health and beauty that our modern society values so much, and is really worth so little, our role in the community changes to one of guidance.It can be a difficult transition. Shed the superficial values and realize that the generations that have preceded us, if we are so lucky as to have them around, have a worth that is much more than we can see.

Meditaton **Ansuz** our ancestral god.

Notes

Hymiskvitha 41

The mighty one came	to the council of gods,
And the kettle he had	that Hymir's was;
So gladly their ale	the gods could drink
In Ægir's hall	at the autumn-time.

Thor has returned with a kettle big enough for Aegir to brew his mead. The association of the ensuing feast with autumn, I believe, is carried forward today. The long hot days of summer are over and the seasons to enjoy family and friends are here. The community and the feast have been with us for a long, long time. Note all the holidays the various peoples of the earth have at this time of the year. Let's enjoy them as they were meant to be.

Notes

_____

_____

_____

_____

_____

_____

_____

_____

_____

Lokasenna 2
Eldir spake:
"Of their weapons they talk, and their might in war,
The sons of the glorious gods;
From the gods and elves who are gathered here
No friend in words shalt thou find."

Our deeds define us and allow us to maintain a good standing in our community. The absence of that community for Loki, even though caused by the strife he himself has stirred up, troubles the mischief maker. He feels he deserves to be let in and that he is worthy of the company of the glorious Gods, when in fact he is not. In Asatru we have a community that is worth belonging to. If we want to be a part of it, it is important to make the effort to be a part of it. Our deeds should reflect this desire to align ourselves with good and worthy folk and not just to show off to bolster a false ego.

Meditate on **Isa** to slow things down so we may make an honest appraisal of ourselves

Notes
_____
_____
_____
_____
_____
_____
_____
_____
_____
_____

Hovamol 36
Better a house,   though a hut it is,
A man is master at home;
A pair of goats and a patched-up roof
Are better far than begging.

Your home is a safe place where you can be yourself, not subject to all the norms you are forced to deal with at work and/or school or even at the shopping mall. Here in our homes we are the master, and here is where the truly important work of self and raising children occurs. This is our way and it is worth defending.

Notes

_____

_____

_____

_____

_____

_____

_____

_____

_____

Skirnismol 39
Gerth spake:
"Find welcome rather,   and with it take
The frost-cup filled with mead;
Though I did not believe   that I should so love
Ever one of the Wanes."

Upon realizing the truth of her condition in the world, Gerth has a moment of clarity when generosity and hospitality become the hallmark of her greeting. Her reluctance and doubt are typical of those new to faith and some type of possible enlightenment, but her courage prevails. As these new sets of principles begin to emerge and take root in her life, her growth and change are just nine nights away. Just as a child lives in the womb for nine months, Gerth's symbolic period of waiting also has a meaning. Anything worth having is worth waiting for.

Meditate on **Dagaz** our awakening.

Notes
_____
_____
_____
_____
_____
_____
_____
_____
_____
_____

Midyear/June

Moderation

Hovamol 11
A better burden   may no man bear
For wanderings wide than wisdom;
Worse food for the journey   he brings not afield
Than an over-drinking of ale.

My uncle would often say when invited to have a drink, "I'm a long way from home to be getting into trouble." When we venture forth, be it in the spirit of adventure on a family vacation or just driving to work, there are millions of other people who are not paying attention to anything going on around them, or they are paying attention to see who they can take advantage of. Our way of life demands that we take possession of life and be responsible for the quality it. There are many who depend upon us whether we know it or not. There are plenty of times for us to relax and enjoy the fine things in life. In the midst of our wanderings is not one of them.
Meditate on **Raidho**, and the journey we are all on.

Notes
_____
_____
_____
_____
_____
_____
_____
_____
_____
_____

Hovamol 12
Less good there lies   than most believe
In ale for mortal men;
For the more he drinks the less does man
Of his mind the mastery hold.

While many of us might agree that overindulgence in a night's drinking may be harmful to us, this realization oft times does little to curb a person's appetite for it. Some people, enjoying the new-found freedom of Asatru and the absence of the guilt we had been burdened with from our Christian days, may be tempted to go just a little too far. But the words of the high one are clear. It is possible to lose ourselves in the cups and mugs from which we drink. The Nine Noble Virtues do not work so well when a person is in his cups. Drink and be merry, but believe that there is more to this life than strong drink. We cannot espouse a proud heritage from beneath a barstool.

Notes

_____

_____

_____

_____

_____

_____

_____

_____

_____

_____

Hovamol 13
Over beer the bird   of forgetfulness broods,
And steals the minds of men;
With the heron's feathers   fettered I lay
And in Gunnloth's house was held.

There are, it seems, two versions of this tale wherein Odin acquires the Mead of Poetry: one in which he is helped by Gunnlod and one in which he seduces Gunnlod and then deserts her. Odin's quest to garner knowledge for himself, and his three nights of pleasure with Gunnlod, leave a memory for him that he is hard pressed to be rid of. While we have no ability to categorically characterize the manner in which the divine interacts with others of similar kind, we can take note that among men this behavior is damaging – not only to us, but often to many others.
We can only cover up so much with strong drink. Our way of life suggests we avoid those situations to begin with. For if we are to find refuge from grief in our wisdom, what do we do when we fail to learn from our mistakes?
Meditate on **Jera** a focus for us to engage in right action.

Notes

_____

_____

_____

_____

_____

_____

_____

_____

_____

Hovamol 19
Shun not the mead,   but drink in measure;
        Speak to the point or be still;
For rudeness none   shall rightly blame thee
        If soon thy bed thou seekest.

We have read the warnings about a liberal appetite for alcohol, but alcohol is a central point in many of our ceremonies. We have no need to fear it. And as to that little voice in your head that wonders, "What if I miss something fun?" or says, "This is such a good time I wish it would last a little longer," or even worse, "I can't wait for the weekend so I can get drunk," well, those thoughts are the whispers of a lingering immaturity. At this point in the game of life, and with a solid set of virtues to guide us and to provide us with an identity and a personal sense of value we may not have had before, we can begin to realize there is much more to us and the world than recreational drinking, and we can set it aside and maintain our honor.

Notes
_____
_____
_____
_____
_____
_____
_____
_____
_____
_____

Hovamol 20
The greedy man,   if his mind be vague,
Will eat till sick he is;
The vulgar man,   when among the wise,
To scorn by his belly is brought.

Asatru folk have a definite way of life. We can be deliberate and focused on our life right here and right now. There is no future for forgiveness and the Virtues guide us through most things. But the character of a vague, vulgar man who is lacking in these virtues will be apparent when he is around Asatruar. It will be apparent he is failing in some way. There really is no faking it around men and women who live Asatru.

Meditate on **Ihwaz** Yggdrasil and our place upon it.

Notes

Hovamol 21

The herds know well   when home they shall fare,
And then from the grass they go;
But the foolish man   his belly's measure
Shall never know aright.

I once heard it said that even a dog knows when he has done something
wrong. If he makes a mess on the floor he will leave the room with his
tale between his legs. Cattle and dogs have been trained day in and day
out how their lives are to be conducted. Humanity has been told time and
again, in every religion the world over, of the basic wisdom to live by, and
this teaching gets ignored when it's not convenient. Then with astounding
audacity we wonder why things aren't going right in our lives. Perhaps
this is why the idea of salvation and forgiveness are such fantastic selling
points. If we live Asatru and enjoy it to the fullest, it is possible that we
can avoid getting into those situations altogether. And a new light begins
to shine on us and our lives.

Notes

_____

_____

_____

_____

_____

_____

_____

_____

_____

Hovamol 33
Oft should one make   an early meal,
    Nor fasting come to the feast;
Else he sits and chews   as if he would choke,
    And little is able to ask.

It is common sense to eat a good breakfast. It may mean you have to get up a little earlier and demonstrate some self-discipline, but the benefits stretch far beyond just enjoying a good meal to start your day. Not to make a pig of yourself is simply good manners when enjoying the hospitality of the folk, or of anyone for that matter.

Meditate on **Nauthiz** and be mindful of your necessities.

Notes
_____
_____
_____
_____
_____
_____
_____
_____
_____
_____

Hovamol 90
The love of women   fickle of will
Is like starting o'er ice   with a steed unshod,
A two-year-old restive and little tamed,
Or steering a rudderless   ship in a storm,
Or, lame, hunting reindeer   on slippery rocks.

None of these things can be trusted to be safe. But the love of a woman of virtue – that is treasure worthy of any of the deeds we may find in the sagas or the Eddas. Are you a man worthy of such a treasure? Are you a woman strong enough to love like that? There are so few examples of this in today's convenient society. But if we look around – and we may indeed have to look closely – it does exist. Maybe in Asatru we can find a way to reclaim something so powerful that even our enemies held it in high regard. Tacitus speaks highly of the union between the men and women of Germania. Reclaiming that heritage is a worthy goal indeed.

Meditate on **Mannaz** a rune of mankind and all its potential.

Notes
_____
_____
_____
_____
_____
_____
_____
_____
_____
_____

Hovamol 147
Better no prayer   than too big an offering,
By thy getting measure thy gift;
Better is none   than too big a sacrifice,
So Thunder of old wrote   ere man's race began,
Where he rose on high   when home he came.

Our spiritual development should be reflected in our daily lives. If we go through life accepting gift after gift our ledger will soon appear out of balance. We have an obligation to give as well as to receive. Here we are reminded that our giving should be measured by how much we have received. This is a simple and universal constant. Indeed it is a law. For every action there is an equal and opposite reaction. As we grow spiritually we may become aware that this concept of giving and receiving carries with it the subtle notion that we should feel free to give; there will be a balancing recompense for it – even if it is just a smile.

Meditate on *Gebo* the rune of gifting.

Notes

Voluspa 21

The war I remember,   the first in the world,
When the gods with spears   had smitten Gollveig,
And in the hall   of Hor had burned her,-
Three times burned,   and three times born,
Oft and again,   yet ever she lives.

This verse concerns the love of gold (Gullveig) and the search for hidden knowledge which exerts a fascination for the selfish. When put into this context it becomes clearer that perhaps the Aesir and Odin's wisdom were trying to work in our favor when they attacked Gollveig. It is only when folk try to insert Freya into this, and thrust in Christian attitudes concerning witchcraft and sorcery, that this passage becomes confusing. Like many things in Asatru there is much more to this story than meets the eye.

Notes

Heimskringla
The
vessel was full of mead, which was excessively strong. In the
evening Fjolne, with his attendants, was taken into the adjoining
loft to sleep. In the night he went out to the gallery to seek a
certain place, and he was very sleepy and exceedingly drunk. As
he came back to his room he went along the gallery to the door of
another left, went into it, and his foot slipping, he fell into
the vessel of mead and was drowned.

Alcohol can be an equal opportunity destroyer.

Meditate on **Hagalaz,** radical change

Notes

_____

_____

_____

_____

_____

_____

_____

_____

_____

Heimskringla
In the evening after sunset, as Swegde was going from the drinking-table to his sleeping-room, he cast his eye upon the stone, and saw that a dwarf was sitting under it.

Anyone who's been drinking with a kindred should know that when you see a dwarf after you've been drinking all night, it might be in your best interest to ignore it.

Notes

Heimskringla
Now when King
Agne had got drunk, Skjalv bade him take care of his gold
ornament which he had about his neck; therefore he took hold of
the ornament, and bound it fast about his neck before he went to
sleep.

Once again an over-indulgence and the words of a pretty woman prove to
be too much for the senses of even a King. It costs him his life.

Meditate on **Kenaz** for knowledge.

Heimskringla
"I tell you of a horrid thing,
A deed of dreadful note I sing --
How by false Bera, wicked queen,
The murderous brother-hands were seen
Each raised against a brother's life;
How wretched Alf with bloody knife
Gored Yngve's heart, and Yngve's blade
Alf on the bloody threshold laid.
Can men resist Fate's iron laws?
They slew each other without cause."

There is less good in ale than men suppose. Truer words have seldom been spoken. When mixed with the words of a treacherous woman and an oversized ego a great many foul actions have occurred without cause.

Notes
_____
_____
_____
_____
_____
_____
_____
_____
_____
_____

Heimskringla
The brothers Eric and Jorund became more celebrated by this deed,
and appeared to be much greater men than before.

One great deed does not mean you can accomplish everything. There is
always someone better than you at just about anything. But that does not
mean you should rest on your laurels and not try. We should always be
willing to dare greatly; even if we fail, we will have learned something
and perhaps grown just a little bit.

Meditate on **Raidho**, the journey is what it's all about

Notes
_____
_____
_____
_____
_____
_____
_____
_____
_____
_____

Heimskringla
Now he sacrificed his ninth son, and lived ten years more; but so that he drank out of a horn like a weaned infant. He had now only one son remaining, whom he also wanted to sacrifice, and to give Odin Upsal and the domains thereunto belonging, under the name of the Ten Lands, but the Swedes would not allow it; so there was no sacrifice, and King On died, and was buried in a mound at Upsal. Since that time it is called On's sickness when a man dies, without pain, of extreme old age.

Those things we sometimes so desire usually have a substantial cost, and may not always be the best for us.

Notes

Heimskringla
For there
were many sea-kings who ruled over many people, but had no lands,
and he might well be called a sea-king who never slept beneath
sooty roof-timbers.

This foundation of the Viking Era in the time of sea-kings, while it may
have its romantic qualities, is out of balance.   Living on the sea all the
time doesn't help us much to build something to leave our descendants on
the land.   While great wealth may be accumulated for the king, what of
the men who serve under him?   When it's all said and done, what do they
possess?   Asatru has many facets, like the finest cut gem; if any one of
them is flawed, it mars the whole work.

Meditate on **Perthro**, the lot cup and your fate.

Notes
_____
_____
_____
_____
_____
_____
_____
_____
_____
_____

Sigrdrifumol 6
"Beer I bring thee, tree of battle,
Mingled of strength and mighty fame;
Charms it holds and healing signs,
Spells full good, and gladness-runes."

A champion should always enjoy the celebration. But in order to be the champion, occasionally you must set the charms and spells aside to engage in hard work. This passage represents a well earned reward for daring greatness.

Notes

Fafnismol 11
Fafnir spake:
"The fate of the Norns before the headland
Thou findest, and doom of a fool;
In the water shalt drown if thou row 'gainst the wind,
All danger is near to death."

We know that the day of your passing is set by the Norns, but this is by
no means a good reason to act like a fool. Enjoy and live a full life. Do
those things that will add to your fame. But use both sides of your brain.

Meditate on **Fehu**, the rune of luck and wealth

Notes

Hovamol 25
"Combed and washed   shall the wise man go,
And a meal at morn shall take;
For unknown it is   where at eve he may be;
It is ill thy luck to lose."

All too often we hear of men striving to do magnificent works, for it has been said, "We are our deeds." But let's not forget the simple tasks of taking care of ourselves and making sure we are prepared for the unexpected. This is going to shape a person's first impression of us. Make it a positive one.

Notes

Hovamol 29-30

29. Then sixth I rede thee, if men shall wrangle,
And ale-talk rise to wrath,
No words with a drunken warrior have,
For wine steals many men's wits.

30. Brawls and ale full oft have been
An ill to many a man,
Death for some, and sorrow for some;
Full many the woes of men.

There is just no way to even appear to have any worth if you are falling down drunk and start an argument. Chances are you will lose and you will certainly damage your own reputation.

Meditate on **Algiz** and becoming who you are supposed to be.

Notes
_____
_____
_____
_____
_____
_____
_____
_____
_____
_____

Prose Edda
"The gods are not deserving of reproof because of this work of skill: a good bridge is Bifröst, but nothing in this world is of such nature that it may be relied on when the sons of Múspell go a-harrying."

This is an interesting comment, one that points out very clearly the struggles even the Gods have against nature and the things they have set in motion. It does not stop them from going forward anyway, and it should not stop you.

Notes
_____
_____
_____
_____
_____
_____
_____
_____
_____

Voluspa 51
Surt fares from the south   with the scourge of branches,
    The sun of the battle-gods   shone from his sword;
    The crags are sundered,   the giant-women sink,
    The dead throng Hel-way,   and heaven is cloven.

The sun of the battle-gods shone from his sword: In the middle of summer it's not too hard to imagine how too much of a good thing can be bad for you.

Notes

Voluspa 58
Now Garm howls loud   before Gnipahellir,
The fetters will burst,   and the wolf run free;
Much do I know and more can see
Of the fate of gods,   the mighty in fight.

In a tale of destruction on such a scale as this, only so much is told that may help us in our lives. There is no need to go on. Our heroes and Gods have been slain and it would appear that all hope is lost as the wolf runs free. We know they were "mighty in fight." How could we in Asatru not feel a huge respect for such courage? Foster that feeling; use it in your prayers and blots and sumbels. And turn strong to face the day.

Meditate on **Uruz** the rune of primal strength

Notes
_____
_____
_____
_____
_____
_____
_____
_____
_____

Voluspa 60

The gods in Ithavoll	meet together,
Of the terrible girdler	of earth they talk,
And the mighty past	they call to mind,
And the ancient runes	of the Ruler of Gods.

The remembrance in such a positive light of past generations by fine sons and daughters is something that hopefully will bless us all. Live a life worthy of your descendants' remembrance.

Notes
_____
_____
_____
_____
_____
_____
_____
_____
_____
_____

Voluspa 62

Then the fields unsowed	bear ripened fruit,
All ills grow better,	and Baldur comes back;
Baldur and Hoth dwell	in Hropt's battle-hall,
And the mighty gods:	would you know yet more?

A vision of heaven for us to enjoy: Unsowed fields bear ripened fruit and ills grow better – and perhaps there is an enlightenment of mankind. I always envision a man standing up and shrugging off the burdens he feels he must carry; in this standing up, straight and tall, perhaps he enjoys a glimpse of Baldur himself. Step forward and claim your life in Asatru.

Meditate on **Kenaz** the torch of knowledge.

Notes

Prose Edda
King Gylfi was a wise man and skilled in magic; he was much troubled
that the Æsir-people were so cunning that all things went according to
their will.

We may not be as wise or skilled in magic as King Gylfi, but we should be
assured that all things go the way the Aesir deem. Our ability to go with
the flow of this in spiritual matters and to witness the results in our
physical word, our ability to accept this, is something akin to faith. The
runes give us ability to tap into this so that our own fortunes may be
enlarged. The Gods did not leave us out of the equation. This heritage is
ours to enjoy as well.

Notes
_____
_____
_____
_____
_____
_____
_____
_____
_____

Prose Edda
A hall I know standing   than the sun fairer,
    Thatched with gold   in Gimlé bright;
There shall dwell   the doers of righteousness
    And ever and ever   enjoy delight.

Gimle shall endure the destruction of heaven and earth. I think it might be worthwhile to look into why this is the case. Maybe there is something to be emulated in our lives. We can start by doing the right thing.

Meditate on **Laguz** the ocean or water

Notes

_____

_____

_____

_____

_____

_____

_____

_____

_____

Prose Edda
XX. Then said Gangleri: "Who are the Æsir, they in whom it behooves men to believe?" Hárr answered: "The divine Æsir are twelve." Then said Jafnhárr: "Not less holy are the Ásynjur, the goddesses, and they are of no less authority."

Here we are told of balance; it is not all a pantheon of Gods of war. There is so much to our Gods and Goddesses; I hope it takes an entire lifetime to figure it out.

Notes

_____

_____

_____

_____

_____

_____

_____

_____

_____

_____

Prose Edda
Nor canst thou ever be called a wise man if thou shalt not be able to tell of those great events.

Someday perhaps, after a lifetime of using Asatru in our lives, we will be able to recount these wondrous tales to our children. The fine example of our lives, lives of struggle and triumph, coupled with tales of the struggles and triumphs of the Gods, will help enable our children to carry Asatru forward. Wise men will once again populate the earth.

Meditate on *Inguz* and the divine within us.

Notes

_____

_____

_____

_____

_____

_____

_____

_____

_____

_____

Haymoon/July

Community

Prose Edda
It is truly said that 'It is best to know evil men only by hearsay.'

Time and again in the sagas and Eddas we are told such things. It is of no small importance; sometimes even the slightest association with "evil men" will affect you and your life in more ways than one.

Meditate on **Thurisaz** and your defense against such people.

Notes

_____

_____

_____

_____

_____

_____

_____

_____

_____

Prose Edda
Odin was the cleverest of all, and from him all the others learned their arts and accomplishments; and he knew them first, and knew many more than other people.

I have always felt we should emulate Odin in this. He is demonstrating to us how to best to enable the success of others. What better way can there be to build a good strong community around you than to learn, teach, and share so that others may enjoy an Asatru life as well.

Notes
_____
_____
_____
_____
_____
_____
_____
_____
_____
_____

Prose Edda
He spoke everything in rhyme, such as now composed, which we call
scald-craft. He and his temple priests were called song-smiths, for from
them came that art of song into the northern countries.

The beauty and power of the spoken word, along with the lyrical
attributes of scald-craft mentioned here, helped build a community that
we – even today after thousands of years – still find worthy to emulate.

Meditate on **Ihwaz** the yew as a symbol of the vertical axis of becoming
who you are supposed to be.

Notes

_____

_____

_____

_____

_____

_____

_____

_____

_____

Prose Edda
Over all Swithiod the people paid Odin a scatt or tax -- so much on each
head; but he had to defend the country from enemy or disturbance, and
pay the expense of the sacrifice feasts for a good year.

Some folks argue against the fees or dues we pay to the organizations to
which we belong. But the willing payments to these organizations go a
long way in helping others and sustaining a centerpoint, if you will, for
our way of life.

Notes

Hovamol 34

Crooked and far   is the road to a foe,
Though his house on the highway be;
But wide and straight is the way to a friend,
Though far away he fare.

It really does take a lot of effort to focus on your enemies and the people you dislike. It's so much healthier for all of us if we build broad avenues to our friends with social media, a personal visit, a letter, or a phone call. If we build these bridges strong, our community cannot help but thrive.

Meditate on **Wunjo** and joy of a fellowship of like minds.

Notes

_____

_____

_____

_____

_____

_____

_____

_____

_____

Vafthruthnismol 2
Frigg spake:
"Heerfather here   at home would I keep,
Where the gods together dwell;
Amid all the giants   an equal in might
To Vafthruthnir know I none."

Frigga in her capacity as Odin's consort and undoubtedly the queen of
Asgard gently reminds Odin of his place in the community of the Aesir. I
should always strive to be a welcome member of the community to which
I belong, be it a local kindred or a national organization. That community
and fellowship help us all pull through and succeed as one.

Notes
_____
_____
_____
_____
_____
_____
_____
_____
_____
_____

Prose Edda
In his days were peace and plenty, and such good years, in all respects,
that the Swedes believed Njord ruled over the growth of seasons and the
prosperity of the people.

To do wonderful things and help others to build a good life for
themselves: This can be said to be the flip side of the great coin of life,
where the obverse is to be a champion on the battlefield. Have you done
either to the extent an entire community will mourn for you? There are
few activities in life more rewarding that enabling the success of those
around you. Maybe it will be just one person whom we affect that much,
but if we do our best for that person, we will have meant the world to
them.

Meditate on **Mannaz** the rune of mankind and the touch of the divine that
resides within our collective consciousness.

Notes
_____
_____
_____
_____
_____
_____
_____
_____
_____
_____

Hovamol 63
To question and answer   must all be ready
Who wish to be known as wise;
Tell one thy thoughts,   be beware of two,-
All know what is known to three.

The halves of this two-part stanza at first glance appearto be unrelated. If we think about it, though, we find they are tied together. In Asatru we engage in windy arguments and come away friends, having taken each other's measure; but if we get carried away and start to run off at the mouth about some wild flight of fancy or past indiscretion, all of it will be for naught. Whatever esteem we may have built can be destroyed in a second with a liberal tongue.

Notes

_____

_____

_____

_____

_____

_____

_____

_____

_____

Hovamol 66
Too early to many a meeting I came,
And some too late have I sought;
The beer was all drunk,   or not yet brewed,
Little the loathed man finds.

Common courtesy suggests that if you show up early you should be prepared to help; if your ego is so out of control that you are consistently late, you should also be prepared to deal with it. There just might not be so much to share, and little will you find in the way of conversation once the work is done.

Meditate on **Ehwaz** and all that the horse represents as a symbol of teamwork.

Notes

_____

_____

_____

_____

_____

_____

_____

_____

_____

Hovamol 69
All wretched is no man,   though never so sick;
Some from their sons have joy,
Some win it from kinsmen,   and some from their wealth,
And some from worthy works.

All of us have a role to play in the building of this worthy way of life we call Asatru.

Notes

_____

_____

_____

_____

_____

_____

_____

_____

_____

_____

Prose Edda
Then began in his days the Frode-peace; and then there were good seasons, in all the land, which the Swedes ascribed to Frey, so that he was more worshipped than the other gods, as the people became much richer in his days by reason of the peace and good seasons.

Once again we see the greatness of peace building and strengthening a community. Perhaps we should spend a little more time building peace and prosperity within ourselves.

Meditate on **Laguz**, water or ocean a substance which connects us all.

Notes
_____
_____
_____
_____
_____
_____
_____
_____
_____
_____

Hymiskvitha 1
Of old the gods   made feast together
And drink they sought   ere sated they were;
Twigs they shook,   and blood they tried:
Rich fare in Ægir's   hall they found.

The description of the feast of the Gods in Aegir's hall is rich with words that hint at mysteries we all wish to understand. Gods are drinking and feasting together. But the references to twigs and blood being put to use imply there was quite a bit more than a simple feast in progress. Even with all that this may suggest, it falls short of conveying to us the magic of the moment. In building communities of our own, we will have the opportunity to enjoy moments of friendship and conviviality with our kin such as this one. The next time you find yourself in a situation such as this, remember this passage, look around you, and feel the moment. These familiar memories of folk and friends represent a magic all their own.

Notes

_____

_____

_____

_____

_____

_____

_____

_____

_____

_____

Heimskringla

Domald took the heritage after his father Visbur, and ruled over
the land. As in his time there was great famine and distress,
the Swedes made great offerings of sacrifice at Upsal. The first
autumn they sacrificed oxen, but the succeeding season was not
improved thereby. The following autumn they sacrificed men, but
the succeeding year was rather worse. The third autumn, when the
offer of sacrifices should begin, a great multitude of Swedes
came to Upsal; and now the chiefs held consultations with each
other, and all agreed that the times of scarcity were on account
of their king Domald, and they resolved to offer him for good
seasons, and to assault and kill him, and sprinkle the stalle of
the gods with his blood. And they did so.

A fine portrayal of leading by example. If anyone is to fall upon the
sword to maintain honor it should be leader first.

Meditate on **Tiwaz**, a rune of justice and sacrifice

Notes

_____

_____

_____

_____

_____

_____

_____

_____

_____

_____

Hovamol 155
An eighth I know,   that is to all
Of greatest good to learn;
When hatred grows   among heroes' sons,
I soon can set it right.

Here we see a spell that can set right the imagined wrongs between the sons of heroes. Sons need their fathers and their heroes, and I have a responsibility to ensure that my sons never feel they have to prove a thing to me. If I have done my best to lead by example, and summoned the courage to examine myself for faults and correct them as best as I can, perhaps my sons will follow suit. If I have done my best, hopefully my sons will not fall victim to those petty emotions which typically fuel such ego-driven hatreds between men. Having said that, perhaps the greatest good to know, is to know thyself.

Notes

_____

_____

_____

_____

_____

_____

_____

_____

_____

Grettir's Saga
By old use and wont these two neighbours should have gone riding together; so Bersi set out and came to Muli, but when he got there Thord was gone.

The Havamal tells us to use the road to a friend's house often and to be hesitant to break a friendship. Both of these precepts are alluded to here, and we get the inkling of an idea that things may not go well for one of the two neighbors in this story. The point is that Asatru is a way of life; we do not really have the option to pick and choose the stanzas we want to apply to our lives. It all ties together. I have to wonder: Am I doing my best to tie it all together and enjoy the blessings of a fine heritage?

Meditate on **_Sowilo_** as a rune of success.

Notes
_____
_____
_____
_____
_____
_____
_____
_____
_____
_____

Saga of Eric the Red

The women then made a ring round about, while Thorbiorg sat up on the spell-dais. Gudrid then sang the song, so sweet and well that no one remembered ever before to have heard the melody sung with so fair a voice as this. The sorceress thanked her for the song, and said: "She has indeed lured many spirits hither, who think it pleasant to hear this song, those who were wont to forsake us hitherto and refuse to submit themselves to us. Many things are now revealed to me which hitherto have been hidden, both, from me and from others."

This is only part of a wonderful description of the importance of women in our society. The gathering of female folk, with a song and a prophecy by those who know, was anintegral part of our ancestral way of life and every bit as important as a man's ability to fight. It was the cement that kept our communities strong.

Notes

_____
_____
_____
_____
_____
_____
_____
_____
_____

Saga of Viga Glum

"I have been in several of the best dwellings here in Eyjafirth, and I have seen none so good as this; but the hangings for your hall are not such as to surpass those of other people." So saying, he took from his chests a set of hangings of such quality that no better had ever come to Iceland, and gave them to Ingiald, who thanked him; and a friendly feeling was now established between them.

This show of gifting in recompense for fine hospitality is as fine a way for men to establish bonds of community as may be found. I find that the openness of Asatru is refreshing in this day and age. Open minds, open hearts, and open homes to folk of good character – these are the makings of a world I would want to raise my daughter in, and I intend to do my best to make this happen.

Meditate on *Gebo* the rune for gift.

Notes
_____
_____
_____
_____
_____
_____
_____
_____
_____
_____

Vafthruthnismol
Vafthruthnir spake:
15. "Speak forth, Gagnrath,   if there from the floor
Thou wouldst thy wisdom make known;
What name has the river   that 'twixt the realms
Of the gods and the giants goes?"

Othin spake:
16. "Ifing is the river   that 'twixt the realms
Of the gods and the giants goes;
For all time ever   open it flows,
No ice on the river there is."

In all the ancient high mythologies the symbolism of the river is important to understand. It represents to simple men a boundary which they may not be able to cross. Ilfing is important because there is never any ice on it. If we look back in time thousands of years, we see men crossing bridges of ice to find new lands. So it's easy to understand where the significance of crossing rivers comes from as well as the daunting possibility of having to cross one that never has any ice. Instead of waiting for the right time, we will be forced to take action to improve ourselves in preparation for the next world. But we are not alone, and the Gods understand the challenge. The protector of mankind, Thor, sets for us an example by crossing several rivers to attend daily council with the Gods. If we believe in the Gods, we can believe in ourselves and cross those boundaries which seem to hinder our development.

Notes
_____
_____
_____
_____
_____
_____
_____
_____
_____

Heimskringla
But as soon as men fell in the
Danish army other men hastened from the country to fill their
places, and also all the vessels in the neighborhood joined
them. The battle ended with the fall of Ottar and the greater
part of his people.

This illustrates the prime reason a sense of community was developed.
To implement that in our society today, we have to ask ourselves: Do we
do our best to look out for other Asatruars in our area? Do we help them
out with work, food, and our own two hands when things may not be
going so well for them? Do we share our success with them and
encourage them to go on and do even better than ourselves?

Meditate on **Berkano**, the birch goddess of growth and renewal.

Notes

_____

_____

_____

_____

_____

_____

_____

_____

_____

_____

Baldrs Draumar 1

Once were the gods   together met,
And the goddesses came   and council held,
And the far-famed ones   the truth would find,
Why baleful dreams   to Baldur had come.

The Aesir look out for one another. In our efforts to follow their lead, we should always be aware of the need to look out for one another.

Notes

_____

_____

_____

_____

_____

_____

_____

_____

_____

_____

Heimskringla
Onund had roads made through all Sweden, both through
forests and morasses, and also over mountains; and he was
therefore called Onund Roadmaker. He had a house built for
himself in every district of Sweden, and went over the whole
country in guest-quarters.

Before you assume the mantle of leadership, be aware that you will then
have the responsibility to develop the spiritual and material conduits that
will foster the advancement of our folk.

Meditate on *Uruz* and the strength necessary to be a leader.

Notes

_____

_____

_____

_____

_____

_____

_____

_____

_____

Laxdaela Saga
Unn spoke to her men and said: "Now you shall be rewarded for all your work, for now I do not lack means with which to pay each one of you for your toil and good-will."

The saga tells that these men traveled from Scotland to the Orkney Isles, to the Faroe Islands, and then to Iceland, where Unn built her wealth and her lands. When the time came and she was able, she rewarded them all. In building a strong community we should never shirk our responsibilities as leaders or as workers. Those roles will change time and again, even on a daily basis. Knowing when to carry out either role is what makes a person a cornerstone of their community. It's what makes that community into something another would want to be a part of.

Notes
_____
_____
_____
_____
_____
_____
_____
_____
_____
_____

Laxdaela Saga

He was a very big, strong man, and one not willing to give in even in face of some odds; and for the reason that he was most overbearing, and would never make good what he had misdone, he had had to fly from West-over-the-sea, and had bought the land on which he afterwards lived.

There are some who seem to be gifted with such a strong desire to be right and succeed in their endeavors that they fail to see the damage done to their standing in the community by their headstrongness. We see this type of person in the sagas as berserkers with no wars to fight, and in today's world as bullies in school. These people usually fail to see how they are perceived, and typically develop resentments towards other for problems of their own making. They are not as valued in a community as they could be or as they think they are. Our challenge, in a way of life that can at times be tilted towards the warrior mentality, is to avoid this and keep the Nine Noble Virtues in balance within ourselves.

Meditate on **Kenaz** for knowledge of self

Notes

Laxdaela Saga
Wise men set great store by people in outlying fishing-stations living peacefully together, and said that it would be unlucky for the fishing if there was any quarrelling; and most men gave good heed to this.

The simple, hard-working communities of people, acting with sole idea in mind of surviving in the manner they best knew how, kept things in perspective. In today's society, with its constant barrage of information telling us that this is important or that thing is worthwhile, it is easy to get lost in the trivia. Reality television is an example of this. As the paragraph says, "wise men give heed to this." Keep focused on what is important – for yourself, your family, and your community.

Notes
_____
_____
_____
_____
_____
_____
_____
_____
_____

Laxdaela Saga
"This is clear, that you will not by peaceful consent allow any man to have the enjoyment of your wealth."

The concept of enjoying one's own wealth seems to have been forgotten by most people. With such a large number of folks so dependent on a hand from the government, we have an obligation to set an example and possibly even create an environment where folks can begin again to earn for themselves. We should use our wealth to build great things in order that others may have an opportunity to put their skills to use.

Meditate on **Fehu**, and luck and wealth are combined in one rune.

Notes
_____
_____
_____
_____
_____
_____
_____
_____
_____
_____

Skirnismol 24
Sigurth spake:
"Unknown it is, when all are together,
(The sons of the glorious gods,)
Who bravest born shall seem;
Some are valiant who redden no sword
In the blood of a foeman's breast."

Having just slain a dragon, Sigurth has a new-found confidence, but it doesn't make him a braggart. He realizes that he is part of a greater whole. He is a champion to be sure, but realizes that there are other ways to win renown for oneself.

Notes

Fafnismol 13
Fafnir spake:
"Of many births the Norns must be,
Nor one in race they were
Some to gods, others to elves are kin,
And Dvalin's daughters some."

This ancient dragon shares a very important insight to us concerning the Norns. They are all daughters, and there are more than three it would seem. This could be a late developing idea with regards to the lore. But it is significant that the Norns come from different races – Gods, dwarves and elves – all of which have something to contribute to men. Maybe we should take a closer look at this in our lives as well.

Meditate on **Raidho**, the journey and the roles the Norns play in that.

Notes
_____
_____
_____
_____
_____
_____
_____
_____
_____
_____

Sigrdrifumol 23
Then first I rede thee, that free of guilt
Toward kinsmen ever thou art;
No vengeance have, though they work thee harm,
Reward after death thou shalt win.

This may well be the only instance where it is even suggested that we turn the other cheek. There is good reason for this exception to the general rule of an eye for an eye: No one ever wins an argument with a family member.

Notes
_____
_____
_____
_____
_____
_____
_____
_____
_____
_____

Egil's Saga
It was his wont to rise up early, and then go round among his laborers or
where his smiths were, and to overlook his stalk and fields, and at times
he would talk with such as needed his counsel, and good counsel he could
give in all things, for he was very wise.

In building a community, there is always a need for a leader such as this
man: someone who rises early, has worked hard to earn his place, and now
enjoys his duty to oversee and provide guidance. In short, he seems to do
his best for the place he is in his life. He not only accepts his
responsibilities for his own person, but also offers to help others to ensure
their success. This is a formula we can all do our best to emulate, and I'm
certain it's one that works on a great many levels. Indeed I'm sure it
works at every level by which we judge the wealth and the strength of a
community.

Meditate on **Ansuz**, the rune of Odin

Notes
_____
_____
_____
_____
_____
_____
_____
_____
_____
_____

Hymiskvitha 41

The mighty one came   to the council of gods,
And the kettle he had   that Hymir's was;
So gladly their ale   the gods could drink
In Ægir's hall   at the autumn-time.

The Lay of Hymikvitha begins and ends with a council of the Gods. In between it outlines a few great feats worthy of the tales around them. In our own world, each day we work hard and stay the course as best we can along the lines of the Nine Noble Virtues, but in the morning and in the evening we should always remember to follow this example of the Gods as well, and that is to try and be part of the community. No matter what is going on, we ought to make an effort, to reach out to the folk and our families. That community and fellowship reinvigorates us in our beliefs and provides a safe harbor when times are tough.

Notes

_____

_____

_____

_____

_____

_____

_____

_____

_____

Hymiskvitha

To join their company, if they will have me, seems to me most desirable;
these men are in far better case than all others in the land. And 'tis told me
of the king that he is most generous in money gifts to his men, and not
slow to give them promotion and to grant rule to such as he deems meet
for it. Whereas I hear this about all that turn their backs upon him and
pay him not homage with friendship, that they all become men of nought,
some flee abroad, some are made hirelings.

Napoleon is known to have once stated, "Give me enough ribbon and I
shall conquer the world." This is referring the lengths a soldier will go to
and the hardships he will endure to pin a ribbon to his chest. The king in
this story likewise understands the simple concept that people want to be
visibly rewarded in front of their peers. A public pat on the back goes a
long way toward building those strong bonds so essential to creating a
community of folk who will survive. Be sure to thank the friends who
support and encourage you.

Meditate on **Othala** our ancestral lot.

Notes

Harvest/ August

Indicviduality
_____

Grouagaldr 13
"Then eighth will I chant thee, if ever by night
Thou shalt wander on murky ways:
Yet never the curse of a Christian woman
From the dead shall do thee harm."

The eighth blessing of the Grouagaldr is not a guard against the elements
or men, but rather against the esoteric. Our ways are different from those
of the big three religions and perhaps we are not smiled upon by them.
They may even laugh in our face, once. But this is who we are and we
need never be ashamed of it. Our ancestors enjoyed this way of life long
before the blip of Christianity occurred on the timeline of history, and it
will continue long after. Stay true to yourself.

Meditate on **Dagaz** the rune of the dawn, the dawn of our way of life.

Notes

Njal's Saga
"Will thine honour be greater there than here?" asks the king.

"No, it will not," said Hrut; "but every one must win the work that is set before him."

We all have a path in life; would that we could all be so lucky as to be as sure of it as Hrut. He has enjoyed a good life of comfort and high adventure, but now it is time to attend to the matters of life in his home. As we all must.

Notes
_____
_____
_____
_____
_____
_____
_____
_____
_____
_____

Hovamol 37
Better a house,   though a hut it be,
A man is master at home;
His heart is bleeding   who needs must beg
When food he fain would have.

A truly crushing blow in life is to have and then lose those things which we all deem so important, to suffer such a blow that one would give up and decide, "Maybe it's just better to beg instead." One in that condition would be a man with a hurt that is truly bleeding.

Meditate on **Sowilo** and let the sun shine upon your success.

Notes
_____
_____
_____
_____
_____
_____
_____
_____
_____
_____

Hovamol 57
A brand from a brand   is kindled and burned,
    And fire from fire begotten;
And man by his speech   is known to men,
    And the stupid by their stillness.

As a fire starts out slowly, so also does a man's life. His deeds become greater and greater just like a fire, until at some point the flame begins to dwindle. To have reached that point and not done anything worthy of talking about is something we must never let happen to ourselves or our children.

Notes

Njal's Saga
He had spent much of his time in seafaring (as a Chapman) and so lucky
was he that he always made the harbor he aimed at.

There are many ways a man or woman can claim fame, fame that will
outlast them. Do what you are tasked to do, to the best of your ability,
every time. That effort in and of itself will set you above most people.

Meditate on **Inguz**, the god seed within us

Notes

_____

_____

_____

_____

_____

_____

_____

_____

_____

Hovamol 65
A man must be watchful   and wary as well,
    And fearful of trusting a friend
Oft for the words   that to others one speaks
    He will get but an evil gift.

Just because we see someone in Asatru it doesn't necessarily mean we
offer them a free pass and expose ourselves like an open book. People
have failings in life, gossip being a particularly dangerous one. Until such
time as I've really taken the measure of a man, there are some things I
simply will not talk about in front of him. Similarly, if we have been
taken into the confidence of someone, we have an obligation to respect
that and not share it with others. Asking forgiveness after the damage of
character assassination has been accomplished is not how we live.

Notes
_____
_____
_____
_____
_____
_____
_____
_____
_____

Hovamol 71
The lame rides a horse,   the handless is herdsman,
The deaf in battle is bold;
The blind man is better   than one that is burned,
No good can come of a corpse.

Sometimes it may appear that the overriding emphasis in Asatru is upon the bold and powerful warrior. While this has been a part of our heritage, we make a mighty mistake in trying to contain the boundless spiritual energy of Asatru within those limitations. All of the folk have something to contribute, even if they have what society may consider a debilitating weakness. There is something you can do. Do it. The emotional dividends you will receive in just helping others with the same condition offer us the chance to grow beyond the pain and prevent us from letting the injury become our identity.

Meditate on **Berkano**, the birch goddess and new beginnings.

Notes

_____

_____

_____

_____

_____

_____

_____

_____

_____

_____

Hovamol 76
Cattle die, and kinsmen die,
And so one dies one's self;
But a noble name will never die,
If good renown one gets.

The moniker I so casually bandy about in conversation, and the heritage I wish to claim because of it, have a greatness all their own. This was not my doing. My name was made into what it is by generations of men, some of them better than me, of my blood. I have an enormous responsibility to embrace it, make it better, and pass it on untarnished. If I have done the job I am supposed to have done in improving myself and setting the example for my sons, perhaps they will do so as well.

Notes
_____
_____
_____
_____
_____
_____
_____
_____
_____
_____

Kormak's Saga
"Surf on a rock-bound shore of the sea-king's blue domain -
Look how it lashes the crags, hark how it thunders again!
But all the din of the isles that the Delver heaves in foam
In the draught of the undertow glides out to the sea-gods' home.
Now, which of us two should test? Is it thou, with thy heart at ease,
Or I that am surf on the shore in the tumult of angry seas?
- Drawn, if I sleep, to her that shines with the ocean- gleam,
- Dashed, when I wake, to woe, for the want of my glittering dream."

A strong man sharing his heart does not minimize his greatness. Like this
wonderful poem, it hints at something greater.

Meditate on **Algiz**, the elk, the beautiful master of the forest.

Notes

_____

_____

_____

_____

_____

_____

_____

_____

_____

Hovamol 83
By the fire drink ale,   over ice go on skates;
Buy a steed that is lean, and a sword when tarnished,
The horse at home fatten,   the hound in thy dwelling.

The simple pleasures of life are still worthy of enjoying, and maybe gratitude forand enjoyment of those simple things please the Gods as well.

Notes
_____
_____
_____
_____
_____
_____
_____
_____
_____
_____

Hovamol 93
Fault for loving let no man find
Ever with any other;
Oft the wise are fettered,   where fools go free,
By beauty that breeds desire.

The greatest stories in the sagas have a common thread of love woven throughout the wondrous tapestry. Wherever we find love in our lives, shouldn't we also consider it worthy of celebration? Our favorite heroes and Gods have sprung from these unions. It is my sincere hope that today some aspect of love makes your life a little brighter.

Meditate on **Nauthiz**, the need fire and the need for love in our lives.

Notes

_____
_____
_____
_____
_____
_____
_____
_____
_____
_____

Hovamol 94
Fault with another   let no man find
for what touches many a man;
Wise men oft   into witless fools
Are made by mighty love.

Men and women have always sacrificed things for the sake of love. This
sacrifice, the letting go of those things which hinder us, to make us
worthy of the love we wish to accept, hasthe potential to make us much
more than we already are.

Notes
_____
_____
_____
_____
_____
_____
_____
_____
_____
_____
_____

Hovamol 95
The head alone knows   what dwells near the heart,
A man knows his mind alone;
No sickness is worse   to one who is wise
Than to lack the longed-for joy.

If we spend all of our time working to gain knowledge, and much energy
in the pursuit being considered wise, there will be the occasional
stumbling block. In this pursuit of wisdom we can easily shortchange
ourselves by denying ourselves the loving touch of someone worthwhile.
This is a curse I would not wish on anyone.

Meditate on *Jera* and a harvest of right action

Notes
_____
_____
_____
_____
_____
_____
_____
_____
_____
_____

Hovamol 119
I rede thee, Loddfafnir!   and hear thou my rede,-
Profit thou hast if thou hearest,
Great thy gain if thou learnest:
An evil man   thou must not let
Bring aught of ill to thee;
For an evil man   will never make
Reward for a worthy thought.

Trust your instincts concerning folk; if they live Asatru it will be
apparent soon enough.

Notes
_____
_____
_____
_____
_____
_____
_____
_____
_____
_____

Hovamol 127
I rede thee, Loddfafnir!   and hear thou my rede,-
Profit thou hast if thou hearest,
Great thy gain if thou learnest:
With a worse man speak not   three words in dispute,
Ill fares better oft
When the worse man wields a sword.

Arguing on the internet is useless.

Meditate on **Thurisaz** as in a wise warrior and a defense from Thor.

Notes

_____

_____

_____

_____

_____

_____

_____

_____

_____

_____

Hovamol 128
I rede thee, Loddfafnir!   and hear thou my rede,-
Profit thou hast if thou hearest,
Great thy gain if thou learnest:
A shoemaker be,   or a maker of shafts,
For only thy single self;
If the shoe is made ill,   or the shaft prove false
Then evil of thee men think.

There are some things you can do for others and some – well, it doesn't matter how it turns out, it just isn't going to be right. Accept the responsibility for yourself and take care of those things you should as best you can.

Notes

_____

_____

_____

_____

_____

_____

_____

_____

_____

Hovamol 129
I rede thee, Loddfafnir!   and hear thou my rede,-
Profit thou hast if thou hearest,
Great thy gain if thou learnest:
If evil thou knowest,   as evil proclaim it,
And make no friendship with foes.

In today's world there are insidious ideas that represent a toe-hold for
bigger ideas that are not for us. Don't waste time on them. Build yourself
first, it is the most effective defense you can have against such folk.

Meditate on **Uruz** for the strength you need.

Notes
_____
_____
_____
_____
_____
_____
_____
_____
_____
_____

Hovamol 130
I rede thee, Loddfafnir!   and hear thou my rede,-
Profit thou hast if thou hearest,
Great thy gain if thou learnest:
In evil never   joy shalt thou know,
But glad the good shall make thee.

Live Asatru!

Notes

Hovamol 96
This found I myself,   when I sat in the reeds,
And long my love awaited;
As my life the maiden   wise I loved,
Yet her I never had.

What action or lack thereof has cost us thus dearly? Do we have the
courage to change it?

Meditate on *Tiwaz* for the courage to take action

Notes

_____

_____

_____

_____

_____

_____

_____

_____

_____

_____

Prose Edda
Then he sent Gefion across the sound to the north to discover new
countries; and she came to King Gylve, who gave her a plough gate of
land. Then she went to Jotunheim, and bore four sons to a giant, and
transformed them into a yoke of oxen. She yoked them to a plough, and
broke out the land into the ocean right opposite to Odin's. This land was
called Sealand, and there she afterwards settled and dwelt. Skjold, a son of
Odin, married her, and they dwelt at Leidre.

For 2000 years and probably more women have had a secondary role to
men in the Christian world in which we live; the Muslim world is even
worse. Yet here we have, in our ancient lore, trust in the capabilities of a
female to accomplish great things from Odin himself. She has worked
hard, visited jotuns, and borne sons, and still she is considered worthy to
be wed to a king and live happily ever after. This is one of the things that
make the Germanic folk-soul so valuable:our sense of justice and equality.

Notes

_____

_____

_____

_____

_____

_____

_____

_____

_____

_____

Hovamol 103
Though glad at home,   and merry with guests,
A man shall be wary and wise;
The sage and shrewd,   wide-wisdom seeking,
Must see that his speech be fair.

There is no need to be a braggart in your own home. Deal fairly with your guests and take a minute to enjoy life with the folk.

Maditate on **Perthro**, build luck with your actions not your words.

Notes

_____

_____

_____

_____

_____

_____

_____

_____

_____

Hovamol 115-116
I rede thee, Loddfafnir!   and hear thou my rede,-
Profit thou hast if thou hearest,
Great thy gain if thou learnest:
Beware of sleep   on a witch's bosom,
Nor let her limbs ensnare thee.
Such is her might   that thou hast no mind
For the council or meeting of men;
Meat thou hatest,   joy thou hast not,
And sadly to slumber thou farest.

When a woman's wiles are turned against you, it will take the joy right out of your life. Take the advice and don't waste your time.

Notes

Prose Edda
When sitting among his friends his countenance was so beautiful and
dignified, that the spirits of all were exhilarated by it, but when he was in
war he appeared dreadful to his foes.

Strong, well defined balance. These folk know who he is and what he can
do; there is no need to continually demonstrate it. Confidence in your
abilities will develop a similar success in you as well.

Meditate on **Mannaz** and your place among men.

Notes

_____

_____

_____

_____

_____

_____

_____

_____

_____

Hovamol 148
The songs I know   that king's wives know not,
Nor men that are sons of men;
The first is called help,   and help it can bring thee
In sorrow and pain and sickness.

A powerful song it must be, if not even the finest of women know it. In
all of those things – in our grief, when we are hurt, and when we fall sick
–throughout our lives, it is usually a woman who takes care of men.
Though it may well be common knowledge among the Aesir and Asynjur,
for us it means there is still room to grow.

Notes

_____

_____

_____

_____

_____

_____

_____

_____

_____

Hovamol 166
Long these song   thou shalt, Loddfafnir,
Seek in vain to sing;
Yet good it were   if thou mightest get them,
Well, if thou wouldst them learn,
Help, if thou hadst them.

A worthy goal is laid out for us, along with a promise that things will go just a little smoother, when times are tough, if we keep our eye on the goal. Take this as a suggestion to keep going when times are toughest. There are answers here in Asatru and reasons to keep believing in our faith and way of life.

Meditate on **Issa**, slow things down and concentrate.

Notes

Hovamol 165
An eighteenth I know,   that ne'er will I tell
To maiden or wife of man,-
The best is what none   but one's self doth know,
So comes the end of the songs,-
Save only to her   in whose arms I lie,
Or who else my sister is.

It is amazing to think that such an old, old text has a brief instruction on dealing with the sacred feminine in a man's psyche: Embrace it. This is quite the opposite of Christianity which squashed such ideas, made a woman subservient to her man, and actively killed millions of women in the witch hunts and inquisitions.

Notes

_____
_____
_____
_____
_____
_____
_____
_____

Saga of Viga Glum

So when summer came he got a ship ready for Glum, and put a cargo on board, with much store of gold and silver, and said to him, "I feel sure we shall not see one another again; but certain special gifts I will give you, that is to say, a cloak, a spear, and a sword, which we in this family have put great trust in. Whilst you retain these articles, I expect that you will never lose your honour; but if you part with them, then I have my fears:" and so they separated.

In these days when the accepted notion of how to succeed in this world is to get a college degree, find a good job, and work hard for a long time, it can be difficult at first to reconcile our notion of hard work with this picture of lavish gifts being simply given to a man. But if we read it closely we can see that the decisive, deliberate actions of a man put him in this fantastic position, and the arms given to him allowed him to take even more action. In today's world we are faced with the need to make decisions daily, sometimes hourly. A solid belief in exactly who we are affords us the same opportunity to take decisive, deliberate actions and earn accord for ourselves as well.

Meditate on **Othala**, our ancestral lot and earthly estate.

Notes

_____

_____

_____

_____

_____

_____

_____

_____

Saga of Viga Glum
Ivar exclaimed, "What folly it is to mock men whom we do not know! He has shown in this matter a courage which I doubt if any of us would come up to."

The matter of our individuality should never be settled at the expense of another we have only heard about.

Notes

Saga of Viga Glum
A man's own hand is most to be trusted.

I imagine that the acceptance of this fact will lead to a great deal of peace in a man's life. For if he believes thus, he already knows what he has to do, and does it.

Meditate on **Kenaz**, the torch of knowledge

Notes

_____
_____
_____
_____
_____
_____
_____
_____
_____

Prose Edda

Thus he established by law that all dead men should be burned, and their belongings laid with them upon the pile, and the ashes be cast into the sea or buried in the earth. Thus, said he, every one will come to Valhalla with the riches he had with him upon the pile; and he would also enjoy whatever he himself had buried in the earth. For men of consequence a mound should be raised to their memory, and for all other warriors who had been distinguished for manhood a standing stone; which custom remained long after Odin's time.

These customs are still with us, as a way to remember the deeds of men. Stand in any National Cemetery and you will see row upon row of men who have done great things for their country. A marker on each one represents that man's faith. Mine will have a hammer.

Notes

_____

_____

_____

_____

_____

_____

_____

_____

Prose Edda
To some he gave victory; others he invited to himself; and they reckoned
both of these to be fortunate.

Fortunate indeed, the chance to achieve greatness either coming or going.
There is a lot of freedom in that absence of fear.

Meditate on **Ansuz**, the rune of Odin and the breath of life.

Notes

_____

_____

_____

_____

_____

_____

_____

_____

Shedding/ September

Truth

Alvissmol 8
Ed emm; /"Ask then, Vingthor,   since eager thou art
The lore of the dwarf to learn,
Oft have I fared   in the nine worlds all,
And wide is my wisdom of each."/

Even though we have all studied and read and done our best to learn all we can of our heritage and the faith of our ancestors that does not automatically ensure Asatru will work in our lives. Although Allvis strives to claim something of the divine which he believes he has earned through study and travel, Thor is there to clear the issue up for him. For when even the sun shines upon him he cannot handle it. So it is with the egos of men who believe that they have earned a spot in the sun because they happen to be well versed in the lore. But we have example after example of the Gods themselves achieving greatness and growth only through suffering and enduring until the end. There are no shortcuts.

Notes

_____

_____

_____

_____

_____

_____

_____

_____

_____

Hovamol 84
A man shall trust not   the oath of a maid,
Nor the word a woman speaks;
For their hearts on a whirling wheel were fashioned,
And fickle their breasts were formed.

Until such time as women become the partners of men in marriage, there are a great many other things that are important in their lives, some of them much more important than the strutting of some rooster bragging upon himself to garner favor for the night.

Meditate on **Dagaz** or the dawn of an awakening.

Notes
_____
_____
_____
_____
_____
_____
_____
_____
_____
_____

Hovamol 91
Clear now will I speak,   for I know them both,
Men false to women are found;
When fairest we speak, then falsest we think,
Against wisdom we work with deceit.

As we noticed on the previous page, there is the potential for a little mistrust between the sexes during the courtship. But there comes a time in a couple's relationship when this is no longer the case, and the truth becomes much more important. Do not squander the trust, as it may well prove to be the bedrock of a fantastic and rewarding partnership that we all hope lasts a lifetime.

Notes

_____

_____

_____

_____

_____

_____

_____

_____

_____

Hovamol 92
Soft words shall he speak   and wealth shall he offer
Who longs for a maiden's love,
And the beauty praise   of the maiden bright;
He wins whose wooing is best.

The most promising words to speak to a maiden are simple truths that
emanate from the heart.

Meditate on **Wunjo** the rune of joy.

Notes

_____
_____
_____
_____
_____
_____
_____
_____
_____
_____

Hovamol 102
(Few are so good   that false they are never
To cheat the mind of a man)
Many fair maids,   if a man but tries them,
False to a lover are found;
That did I learn when I longed to gain
With wiles the maiden wise;
Foul scorn was my meed   from the crafty maid,
And nought from the woman I won.

There is nothing more dangerous than the half truth. I can find no good argument for trying to determine the potential for dishonesty in a mate by using such a tactic. In fact the end of this stanza proves it: He ended up with nothing.

Notes

_____

_____

_____

_____

_____

_____

_____

_____

_____

Hovamol 103
Though glad at home,   and merry with guests,
          A man shall be wary and wise;
The sage and shrewd,   wide-wisdom seeking,
          Must see that his speech be fair.

Let's try to avoid diarrhea of the mouth. If we can train ourselves to speak in simple truthful terms, without all the extraneous reasoning we sometimes try to use to explain to people why we believe the way we do, it is possible we can achieve a greater esteem in the eyes of those who may count the most. Winston Churchill's famous speech at Harrow in 1941 conveyed to an entire nation in 43 words the attitude that enabled that nation to persevere through one of the darkest times in its history. Never give in.

Meditate on **Jera**, the harvest of right action

Notes
_____
_____
_____
_____
_____
_____
_____
_____
_____
_____

Hovamol 120
I saw a man   who was wounded sore
By an evil woman's word;
A lying tongue   his death-blow launched,
And no word of truth there was.

They say that sometimes the truth hurts, but lies spoken into existence do damage far beyond what we may intend. If the concepts of Wyrd, Orlog and the symbolic ideas we hold sacred concerning Sumbel mean anything to us, we will avoid such lies as if they are a fire that intends to burn us. It is quite possible that they are. Do your best today to speak the truth.

Notes

_____

_____

_____

_____

_____

_____

_____

_____

_____

_____

Hovamol III
On his ring swore Othin the oath, methinks;
Who now his troth shall trust?
Suttung's betrayal   he sought with drink,
And Gunnloth to grief he left.

The failure to be honest and bold has consequences for the Allfather himself. Why should we think it would be anything less for us?

Meditate on **Perthro**, the lot cup of luck.

Notes

_____

_____

_____

_____

_____

_____

_____

_____

_____

Groagaldr 11
"Then sixth I will chant thee, if storms on the sea
Have might unknown to man:
Yet never shall wind or wave do harm,
And calm is the course of thy boat."

We see this many times explained as a miracle of faith, but in our way of Asatru it is as simple as a mother's love for her son.

Notes

_____

_____

_____

_____

_____

_____

_____

_____

_____

Groagaldr 14
"Then ninth will I chant thee, if needs thou must strive
With a warlike giant in words:
Thy heart good store of wit shall have,
And thy mouth of words full wise."

Even against the angriest of foes, never fear to speak the truth.

Meditate on **Tiwaz** for courage.

Notes

_____

_____

_____

_____

_____

_____

_____

_____

_____

_____

_____

Emperor Julian the Apostate
"For it is in knowledge that the Gods surpass us. And it may well be that with them also what ranks as noblest is self knowledge. In proportion then as they are nobler than we in their essential nature, that self knowledge of theirs is knowledge of higher things." Emperor Julian, The Apostate.   To The Uneducated Cynics

While this is very clearly referring to a different pantheon of Gods than those of Asatru, I believe the same principle holds true. More importantly, it brings to mind the very clear idea that these wonderful works of classical literature from ancient Rome, Greece, Germania, Persia, and India are all Pagan.

Notes

_____

_____

_____

_____

_____

_____

_____

_____

_____

Saga of Viga Glum

"It is very different from what you suppose," said Hreidar; "there are many good fellows there." "Well," replied Ivar, "at any rate that rough and shaggy beast does not look particularly well on the high seat." But when he saw that his brother set great store by Eyiolf he did not speak so strongly as before against Icelanders.

In Asatru we come across may types of folks. Folkish and universalist (as loath as I am to use labels) come to mind first, and differences spread out from there. There are those who use Asatru to foster hate and bolster false ego. There is a reason courage is at the top of the list of virtues. Hreidar stands his ground and speaks the truth, and though it may not change anyone's mind, we should always speak the truth as we see it. This means we must also have the courage to accept when we are wrong and realize it does not diminish us as people if we are, for then we commence to learn and gain wisdom.

Meditate on **Kenaz** the torch of learning and knowledge.

Notes

_____

_____

_____

_____

_____

_____

_____

_____

_____

Prose Edda
Another cause was, that he conversed so cleverly and smoothly, that all
who heard believed him.

There is no trick to speaking the truth.

Notes

Heimskringla
King Dive's son, called Dag, succeeded to him, and was so wise a
man that he understood the language of birds. He had a sparrow
which told him much news, and flew to different countries.

This is a grandson of Rig, and a king in his own right. Rig's visit was a
fourth blessing from the divine as we perceive it. The Gods' interest in
mankind has not waned from the time Odin gave soul and life; Vili gave
wit and sense of touch; and Ve gave countenance, speech, hearing, and
sight. Dag laid claim to this heritage and enjoyed a prosperous rule.
Somewhere in our ancestry there is a heritage for us also to claim. Live a
noble life and claim it.

Meditate on **Othala**, our ancestral lot

Notes
_____
_____
_____
_____
_____
_____
_____
_____
_____
_____

Heimskringla
It was a common saying that King Ingiald had
killed twelve kings, and deceived them all under pretence of
peace; therefore he was called Ingiald the Evil-adviser.

My grandfather used to say, "Behind every great fortune was the shadow of a lie." There are so many ways a person can achieve greatness, it's almost impossible to count. Being evil is not one of the better ones. This paragraph goes on to tell how Ingiald's daughter earned the same moniker. When it is all said and done and your life is over, most of the time the only way the world will perceive your greatness is by the quality of people your children become. To be truthful with them and set an honorable example is, perhaps, one of the finer avenues to greatness a person can follow.

Notes

_____

_____

_____

_____

_____

_____

_____

_____

_____

Sigrdrifumol 4
"Hail to the gods! Ye goddesses, hail,
And all the generous earth!
Give to us wisdom and goodly speech,
And healing hands, life-long."

We hail the Gods and Goddesses and all the generous Earth. If we have wisdom, and goodly speech, and healing hands throughout our lives, imagine the good success we can enjoy and help others to enjoy as well.

Meditate on **Sowilo**, let the sun shine upon our success

Notes
_____
_____
_____
_____
_____
_____
_____
_____
_____

Sigrdrifumol 8
Ale-runes learn, that with lies the wife
Of another betray not thy trust;
On the horn thou shalt write, and the backs of thy hands,
And Need shalt thou mark on thy nails.
Thou shalt bless the draught, and danger escape,
And cast a leek in the cup;
(For so I know thou never shalt see
Thy mead with evil mixed.)

This is a potent combination of wisdom and the runes. When ale is involved it is important that you be protected from evil for that is when we are the weakest.

Notes

Sigrdrifumol 12
Speech-runes learn, that none may seek
To answer harm with hate;
Well he winds and weaves them all,
And sets them side by side,
At the judgment-place, when justice there
The folk shall fairly win.

This is not a turn the other cheek attitude, but a faith in the justice of the time and a belief that the runes will work in our favor.

Meditate on **Algiz** and a connection to the higher self as depicted by the elk in the forest.

Notes

_____

_____

_____

_____

_____

_____

_____

_____

Fafnismol 9
Fafnir spake:
"In all I say dost thou hatred see,
Yet truth alone do I tell;
The sounding gold, the glow-red wealth,
And the rings thy bane shall be."

Even a broken clock is right twice a day. Just because we dislike someone doesn't mean they do not have some bit of wisdom worth sharing. Do not let hate steal this path from you.

Notes

_____

_____

_____

_____

_____

_____

_____

_____

Fanismol 24
Sigurth spake:
"Unknown it is, when all are together,
(The sons of the glorious gods,)
Who bravest born shall seem;
Some are valiant who redden no sword
In the blood of a foeman's breast."

Not all of us are destined for great victories on the battlefield. But this does not diminish the contributions we can make when we stay true to ourselves. We should always consider that we have a worthwhile purpose. The adventure is determining what that is.

Meditate on **_Ehwaz_** the rune of teamwork.

Notes

_____

_____

_____

_____

_____

_____

_____

Fafismol 36
A fifth spake:
"Less wise must be the tree of battle
Than to me would seem the leader of men,
If forth he lets one brother fare,
When he of the other the slayer is."

It is one thing to be a leader in a fight and quite another to lead men. But in both cases you have to first understand yourself and secondly understand your opponent. Sigurth was lucky enough to hear the speech of the birds to learn this lesson. We have to do it the hard way – one more reason the wisdom of the elders is so important, along with our decisive actions to implement decisions and deal with the consequences.

Notes
_____
_____
_____
_____
_____
_____
_____
_____

Reginsmol 23
"A man shall fight not   when he must face
The moon's bright sister   setting late;
Win he shall   who well can see,
And wedge-like forms   his men for the fray."

Form a wedge and don't fight when the sun is setting. Most old soldiers will see the value of this advice. But how can we apply it to our lives and our businesses? Well, we can start by doing just what Sigurth did: he asked an expert.

Meditate on **Inguz** the seed of the divine within each of us.

Notes

Sigrdrifumol 19
Beech-runes are there, birth-runes are there
And all the runes of ale,
And the magic runes of might;
Who knows them rightly and reads them true,
Has them himself to help;
Ever they aid,
Till the gods are gone.

This is a powerful truth for us. Not only have we been blessed by Odin, Vili, and Ve, but in a similar manner we have been blessed by Rig's visit and Gefjon's courtship. The divine courses through our veins, and we have also been blessed with odd looking tools called the runes. Our faith, our work with the runes, and our efforts havebeen supported by the Gods since the beginning. Here we find a solid reason to believe that we have everything we need to thrive and become who we are supposed to be.

Notes

Sigrdrifumol 32
Then eighth I rede thee, that evil thou shun,
And beware of lying words;
Take not a maid, nor the wife of a man,
Nor lure them on to lust.

The situations you can create with a lie will almost always overwhelm you, especially when it comes to relationships. Random lust that has to be satisfied by means of a lie can be an evil thing.

Meditate on **Hagalaz**, the grain of water and its ability to change for the better.

Notes

_____

_____

_____

_____

_____

_____

_____

_____

Sigrdrifumol 8
"He beset me with shields in Skatalund,
Red and white, their rims o'erlapped;
He bade that my sleep should broken be
By him who fear had nowhere found."

There is a school of thought that this story represents a person discovering the feminine or other side of themselves. This theme is mirrored in a great many tales such as Sleeping Beauty. It's not a great leap to look at ourselves and determine if we have shields all around our hearts; we will only awaken when we have enough courage to break through those shields. Something to think about.

Notes

_____

_____

_____

_____

_____

_____

_____

_____

Helreith Bryhildar 13
"Ever with grief and all too long
Are men and women born in the world;
But yet we shall live our lives together,
Sigurth and I. Sink down, Giantess!"

Even at our death, the baser elements of nature – in this case a giantess – try to rob us and our heroes of a rightfully deserved happiness. When faced with betrayal and lies it does indeed seem as if life can drag on forever. But the passing of our lives is not the end. There are many opportunities for new-found joy and happiness after we shed this mortal coil. Valhalla is but one of them.

Meditate on **Berkano**, the rune of growth and new beginnings.

Notes

_____

_____

_____

_____

_____

_____

_____

_____

Egil's Saga
Then answered many who stood by, and all with one mind, that it was a slander of wicked men if such words had been spoken, and Thorolf would be found guiltless. The king said he would prefer to believe this. Then was the king cheerful in all his talk with Thorgils, and they parted friends.

They all answered and all with one mind: This kind of loyalty can only be developed among our folk and friends by brave and generous men, especially today when the truth seems to be inconvenient sometimes.

Notes
_____
_____
_____
_____
_____
_____
_____
_____

Prose Edda
Surtr fares from the south   with switch-eating flame,-
On his sword shimmers   the sun of the War-Gods;
The rock-crags crash;   the fiends are reeling;
Heroes tread Hel-way;   Heaven is cloven.

One of the kennings for Loki is Lopt (fire). The fear and respect with which our ancestors held fire is obvious in our Eddas. It creates and it destroys; fire consumes everything in the simple act of being. But it provides warmth, its ashes provide fertilizer, and new healthy ideas and plants emerge from the devastation it leaves behind. Sometimes magnificent change can be found in our lives as well, in things that we may perceive as the end and as a threat to all that we know. But if our knowledge of the world teaches us anything, it's that everything is a cycle. In all this change we know that the Sons of the War Gods will rise again, in Baldur and Nanna.
Meditate on **Dagaz** the dawn of a new beginning

Notes
_____
_____
_____
_____
_____
_____
_____
_____

Prose Edda
"Just as cold arose out of Nifiheim, and all terrible things, so also all that looked toward Múspellheim became hot and glowing; but Ginnungagap was as mild as windless air, and when the breath of heat met the rime, so that it melted and dripped, life was quickened from the yeast-drops, by the power of that which sent the heat, and became a man's form."

In this description of our creation, we can, if we look closely, see a greater understanding of principles thanmost people today would ascribe to our ancient ancestors. In the absence of electron microscopes and knowledge of biology, they knew that in between the two extremes there is a healthy medium from which a life may grow. The extremes may be savage and primal to be sure, but are something that can be worked and built upon to greater purpose. Our lives are no different. In the chaos that sometimes surrounds us, if we can manage to be still and focus, through our own mighty efforts we may also create a life for ourselves.

Notes

_____

_____

_____

_____

_____

_____

_____

_____

Prose Edda
And this is my belief, that he, Odin, with his brothers, must be ruler of heaven, and earth; we hold that he must be so called; so is that man called whom we know to be mightiest and most worthy of honor, and ye do well to let him be so called.

All of the ancient mythologies and religions of the world show a son becoming better than the father in someway. This provides a ray of hope for us all to believe in. Odin creates the world, it is destroyed, and Baldur returns to perfect it. Each of us has quite a bit of work to do to follow this example. But if our world is to become a place worthy of the efforts that have been put into it, a simple acceptance of this truth is required. That my sons will use my example to become better men and do something fantastic is very important to me. When you are gone, in today's society, one of the few ways a person will determine your worth is the quality of people your children become. May Odin smile upon them.
Meditate on **Laguz** water as common element among us all.

Notes

_____

_____

_____

_____

_____

_____

_____

_____

Hunting/ October

Steadfastness

Hovamol 140
1. (140) I ween that I hung   on the windy tree,
Hung there for nights full nine;
With the spear I was wounded,   and offered I was
To Othin, myself to myself,
On the tree that none   may ever know
What root beneath it runs.

This description of such a lonely, painful state of being can be of some comfort when the spirit is in the same situation. The trials of life – and sometimes they can be battles with the self, dealing with psychological shortcomings or addictions of some sort – can be lonely times, but if we stay the course and maintain our faith we can make it.

Notes

Hovamol 118
I rede thee, Loddfafnir!   and hear thou my rede,-
Profit thou hast if thou hearest,
Great thy gain if thou learnest:
If o'er mountains or gulfs   thou fain wouldst go,
Look well to thy food for the way.

Anytime we plan to stay the course, we should be properly prepared.
Mental, physical, emotional, and spiritual preparation, are all aspects of a
well-rounded individual; all of them are necessary to maintain a
straightforward path in life.

Meditate on **Ansuz** the very breath of Odin.

Notes
_____
_____
_____
_____
_____
_____
_____
_____
_____

Groagaldr 16
"Bear hence, my son, what thy mother hath said,
And let it live in thy breast;
Thine ever shall be the best of fortune,
So long as my words shall last."

Many times I have had to struggle to accomplish tasks set before me. In those times just the simple thought of love from my parents, wife, or children has kept me going through what could be perceived as insurmountable odds. Taking that one step further, there are other kin, the distant divine relatives we hold dear, who are just as interested in our success as our living relatives are.

Notes

_____

_____

_____

_____

_____

_____

_____

_____

_____

_____

Hovamol 143
Then began I to thrive,   and wisdom to get,
I grew and well I was;
Each word led me on   to another word,
Each deed to another deed.

This is a clear stanza that outlines in simple terms the rewards of steadfastness, of sticking with it and seeing it through, whether it is high school or the officers' course, building a tower or cleaning the house. Stick to the task at hand and do the best you can with it. These little victories in your life in general lay a foundation upon which you can depend and from which you can grow into who you are supposed to become.

Meditate on **Jera** and a harvest of right action.

Notes

Svipdagsmol 64
Mengloth spake:
"Welcome thou art, for long have I waited;
The welcoming kiss shalt thou win!
For two who love is the longed-for meeting
The greatest gladness of all."

We see it time and again on the television, and occasionally get to experience it in our lives: the joyous reunion. They have always said that absence makes the heart grow fonder, and to some extent it is true. I believe that as well when I see a slogan that tells me returning to my faith is like coming home. It warms a very special place in my heart and I do feel very welcomed indeed.

Notes
_____
_____
_____
_____
_____
_____
_____
_____
_____
_____

Njal's Saga
"It is pulling a rope against a strong man," said Gunnhillda, "so give him leave to go as best suits him."

If we are behaving as we are supposed to, living the Nine Noble Virtues and enjoying all that life has to offer, others will notice. There is no finer compliment than to receive the blessing of friend or a wife or husband, or even a mother and father, to do as you please because they believe in you

Meditate on **Uruz** the rune of strength.

Notes

_____

_____

_____

_____

_____

_____

_____

_____

_____

Kormac's Saga
"Long I've lived,
And I've let the gods guide me;
Brown hose I never wore
To bring the luck beside me.
I've never knit
All to keep me thriving
Round my neck a bag of worts,
- And lo! I'm living!"

This is a taunt to a man who may well be a mighty warrior. But we have to wonder: is he as mighty as he thinks? Steinar proclaims a belief in himself as well as the Gods, knowing they are all tied together. He ties the use of magic, wearing hose, knitting and/or a bag of worts (magic) to a feminine idea of courage that is most unbecoming in a man. The last line says it all: he has enjoyed a strong faith and a good life and says with celebration, "And lo! I'm living!" Yes indeed he is.

Notes

Honsa-Thori's Saga
Don't do this, Thorvald, said Arngrim, because he is not a good man to help. Besides, you would be setting yourself up against a man who is wise and mighty, and well-liked by everyone.

I see that you envy my receiving his money, said Thorvald, and you begrudge it to me.

Against wise counsel a weaker man is easily swayed by the thought of easy money. Stay true to yourself. Wealth in many forms will come your way if you live the Nine Noble Virtues.

Meditate on **Fehu** the rune of wealth

Notes

_____

_____

_____

_____

_____

_____

_____

_____

_____

Heimskringla
Yrsa was not one of
the slave girls, and it was soon observed that she was
intelligent, spoke well, and in all respects was well behaved.
All people thought well of her, and particularly the king; and at
last it came to this that the king celebrated his wedding with
her, and Yrsa became queen of Sweden, and was considered an
excellent woman.

Everyone starts at the bottom, but if we strive to always become better, if
we persevere in our most difficult tasks and endeavor to do at our best in
good and bad times, it always pays off.

Notes
_____
_____
_____
_____
_____
_____
_____
_____
_____

Heimskringla
"With fiery feet devouring flame
Has hunted down a royal game
At Raening, where King Ingiald gave
To all his men one glowing grave.
On his own hearth the fire he raised,
A deed his foemen even praised;
By his own hand he perished so,
And life for freedom did forego."

Ingiald and his daughter were both considered evil people. But he did understand that when the game is up and it's time to pay the piper you do it with as much honor as you can muster.

Meditate on **Tiwaz**, courage and sacrifice

Notes

Laxdaela Saga

Bjorn, the son of Ketill, answered: "I will make known my wishes at once. I will follow the example of noble men, and fly this land. For I deem myself no greater a man by abiding at home the thralls of King Harald, that they may chase me away from my own possessions, or that else I may have to come by utter death at their hands."

Possessions come and go, but our principles must never waiver. To follow the example of noble men requires strength of character that we may or may not be born with. In the steadfast and earnest desire to emulate people worthy of our admiration lie the roots of our own growth, and the potential for the betterment of ourselves and those around us.

Notes

_____

_____

_____

_____

_____

_____

_____

_____

_____

Laxdaela Saga

But the day after Olaf went to the sleeping bower of Unn, his
grandmother, and when he came into the chamber there was Unn sitting
up against her pillow, and she was dead. Olaf went into the hall after that
and told these tidings. Every one thought it a wonderful thing, how Unn
had upheld her dignity to the day of her death.

If we are to be true leaders, it is our duty to remain resolute in the most
difficult of times. People are moved to do great things on behalf of a man
who is doing his best for others. Not so with the beggar on the corner, one
who has given up on life and is simply waiting to die. It is a true leader
who walks directly into the arms of death with bold dignity after the work
is done.

Meditate on **Thurisaz** the wise warrior

Notes

_____

_____

_____

_____

_____

_____

_____

_____

_____

Fafismol 28
Sigurth spake:
"Better is heart than a mighty blade
For him who shall fiercely fight;
The brave man well shall fight and win,
Though dull his blade may be."

We cannot always be prepared with the very best of things, but we can strive to do our best with what we have. Many times that attitude makes all the difference in the world.

Notes
_____
_____
_____
_____
_____
_____
_____
_____
_____

Sigrdrifumol 3
"Hail, day! Hail, sons of day!
And night and her daughter now!
Look on us here with loving eyes,
that waiting we victory win."

When she awoke, she shared a horn of mead and hailed the day and his sons and the night and her daughters. When we wake up what's the first thing on our mind?

Meditate on **Dagaz**, the rune of the dawn.

Notes
_____
_____
_____
_____
_____
_____
_____
_____
_____

Sigrdrifumol 10
Wave-runes learn, if well thou wouldst shelter
The sail-steeds out on the sea;
On the stem shalt thou write, and the steering-blade,
And burn them into the oars;
Though high be the breakers, and black the waves,
Thou shalt safe the harbour seek.

The gift of the runes, if used properly, will pull us through any storm.

Notes
_____
_____
_____
_____
_____
_____
_____
_____
_____

Fafismol 6
Sigurth spake:
"My heart did drive me, my hand fulfilled,
And my shining sword so sharp;
Few are keen when old age comes,
Who timid in boyhood be."

Sometimes you've got to fight to develop the person you are supposed to be. What wisdom will you share, when you get old, if you've never done anything in life? There is a reason the heart of champion is so respected.

Meditate on **Sowilo** the rune of the sun

Notes
_____
_____
_____
_____
_____
_____
_____
_____
_____

Fafnismol 10
Sigurth spake:
"Some one the hoard shall ever hold,
Till the destined day shall come;
For a time there is when every man
Shall journey hence to Hel."

Surround yourself with "why not" people. Someone is going to be the hero, someone is going to make it big, and someone will enjoy a rich heritage and celebrate a lavish lifestyle. Why shouldn't it be you?

Notes

_____
_____
_____
_____
_____
_____
_____
_____
_____
_____

Fafnismol 19
Sigurth spake:
"Glittering worm, thy hissing was great,
And hard didst show thy heart;
But hatred more have the sons of men
For him who owns the helm."

As free men, we have an obligation to stand tall and speak with courage.
Let's not wait until hatred festers within us like some kind of
cancer. Better that we should stand up for who and what we are on a daily
basis and do our best to prevent tyranny in our lives.

Meditate on **Mannaz** the rune of mankind

Notes

Sigrdrifumol
Sigrdrifa slew Hjalmgunnar in the battle,
and Othin pricked her with the sleep-thorn in punishment for this, and
said that she should never thereafter win victory in battle, but that she
should be wedded. "And I said to him that I had made a vow in my turn,
that I would never marry a man who knew the meaning of fear."

What choice could a being like a Valkyrie have really had in this
situation? To live in defeat, or sleep until a champion arrived. All too
often this also happens to us. We are faced with decisions everyday that
are difficult to deal with, but must be met in order to live in this world,
this society; to keep a job; to maintain good standing. Those feelings we
have, those longings for a chance to achieve greatness, thatlie in our hearts
and dance about the edges of our imagination when we watch a movie or
read a book – that is the sleeping champion within us. Asatru will help
waken that within us that makes us great, that points out that we are God
kin and that there is a heritage for us to claim.

Notes

_____

_____

_____

_____

_____

_____

_____

_____

Reginsmol 20
Hnikar spake:
"Many the signs,   if men but knew,
That are good for the swinging of swords;
It is well, methinks,   if the warrior meets
A raven black on his road."

"Many are the signs, if men but knew." There are few phrases in the Eddas that elicit a more hopeful response within me. It suggests that there is hope for us. The signs are there, just like our Gods; we just need to look.

Meditate on **Kenaz** the torch of knowledge

Notes

Reginsmol 21
"Another it is   if out thou art come,
And art ready forth to fare,
To behold on the path   before thy house
Two fighters greedy of fame."

Being ready to fare forth is a part of our responsibility as men and women. We should not take the large amount of automation in our lives for granted. This verse is about an auspicious omen for a fight, but there are so many other situations besides fighting for which we should be prepared. It's only common sense, and this world today needs a huge injection of common sense. Let's demonstrate the ability of Asatru to do this in ourselves and our lives.

Notes
_____
_____
_____
_____
_____
_____
_____
_____
_____

Sigrdrifumol 35
Battle and hate and harm, methinks,
Full seldom fall asleep;
Wits and weapons the warrior needs
If boldest of men he would be.

Those things that sometimes cause us to lose sleep – anger and fights and hatred and old wounds – if given half a chance will rob us of our full potential.

Meditate on **Algiz** a connection to your higher self.

Notes
_____
_____
_____
_____
_____
_____
_____
_____
_____

Egil's Saga

The king set his own ship in the van, and there the battle was most stubborn, but the end was that king Harold won the victory.

Here is a king leading by example – firm, steadfast, and resolute. There was no promise that he would win the battle, only the courage to step up to the plate and do his best.

Notes

_____

_____

_____

_____

_____

_____

_____

_____

_____

Egil's Saga

Then the king had his men's wounds bound up, and thanked them for their valour, and gave them gifts, adding most praise where he thought it most deserved. He promised them also further honour, naming some to be steersmen, others forecastle men, others bow-sitters. This was the last battle king Harold had within the land; after this none withstood him; he was supreme over all Norway.

King Harold had determined to do this long before. To achieve this – I think it is important to note – instead of becoming drunk with initial success and forgetting how and what he was doing, he continued to promote well earned success in those around him.

Meditate on **Uruz** the rune of primal strength.

Notes
_____
_____
_____
_____
_____
_____
_____
_____
_____

Prose Edda

The sun knew not	where she had housing;
The moon knew not	what might he had;
The stars knew not	where stood their places.
Thus was it ere	the earth was fashioned.

How could anyone, 40,000 years ago, know of the status of the universe before the big bang, without a little help? There are truths to be made evident to us all if we stay the course.

Notes

_____

_____

_____

_____

_____

_____

_____

_____

_____

Voluspa 47

Yggdrasil shakes,	and shiver on high
The ancient limbs,	and the giant is loose;
To the head of Mim	does Othin give heed,
But the kinsman of Surt	shall slay him soon.
How fare the gods?	how fare the elves?
All Jotunheim groans,	the gods are at council;
Loud roar the dwarfs	by the doors of stone,
The masters of the rocks;	would you know yet more?

All those things set in motion long ago groan and roar at the coming doom. Odin's efforts to delay this day have worked in our favor for a long time. Yet Odin knows that against the forces of nature that he himself set in motion, he cannot win. The Gods give council and prepare to meet their glorious doom.

Meditate on **Ansuz** and the inspiration of Odin

Notes

Voluspa 57

The sun turns black,	earth sinks in the sea,
The hot stars down	from heaven are whirled;
Fierce grows the steam	and the life-feeding flame,
Till fire leaps high	about heaven itself.

There is a striking similarity here to our story of creation. It hints at the fact that the men who first told these stories held a vast store of knowledge that we often times fail to give them credit for. In this description is also hope; just as the phoenix rises from the flames, so too out of this primordial mix of steam and flame do we recognize the ingredients for new life.

Notes

_____

_____

_____

_____

_____

_____

_____

_____

_____

Voluspa 59

Now do I see   the earth anew
Rise all green   from the waves again;
The cataracts fall,   and the eagle flies,
And fish he catches   beneath the cliffs.

Just as we have surmised, the earth rises anew. There is the sound of the waves and the cry of the eagle fishing beneath the cliffs. The very mention of a place of in between, the shore of the ocean, where liquid and solid meet, has the power to conjure in our minds heartfelt images of peace and hope. This also we can use in our lives.

Meditate on **Berkano** the rune of new beginnings

Notes

_____

_____

_____

_____

_____

_____

_____

_____

_____

_____

Voluspa 61
In wondrous beauty   once again
Shall the golden tables   stand mid the grass,
Which the gods had owned,   in days of old,
-lacuna- And played at tafle,   would ye know yet more?

Through the absolute toughest of times, death and destruction on a cosmic
scale, they have stayed the course. They did not go quietly into that good
night; they fought with courage the oncoming tide of events. As the
results of their own actions – in this day, in wondrous beauty – they reap
their rewards.

Notes
_____
_____
_____
_____
_____
_____
_____
_____
_____

Voluspa 64
More fair than the sun,   a hall I see,
Roofed with gold,   on Gimle it stands;
There shall the righteous   rulers dwell,
And happiness ever   there shall they have.

None of this comes without sacrifice. But it will come, if we just keep on trying.

Meditate on **Hagalaz** the rune of radical change

Notes

_____

_____

_____

_____

_____

_____

_____

_____

_____

Gripisspo 55
Sigurth spake:
"Now fare thee well!   our fates we shun not;
And well has Gripir   answered my wish;
More of joy   to me wouldst tell
Of my life to come   if so thou couldst."

We have all been given a path to negotiate in life. Some are much more difficult than others. The attitude with which we approach life is the complete opposite of how a Christian might deal with it. Instead of praying and waiting for difficulties to pass, and then giving credit to the holy for what is really the simple passing of time, we walk headlong into such difficulties as arise, secure in the knowledge that we have been created and blessed with everything we need to thrive and survive the environment and situation we happen to be in. In our steadfast attempt to live a noble life either we will succeed and be hailed as the victor, or we will celebrate a glorious death. Both of these are good things.

Notes
_____
_____
_____
_____
_____
_____
_____
_____
_____

Fogmoon/ November

Loyalty

Prose Edda
Bravely Thor fought for Ásgard
And the followers of Odin.

A fine, clear declaration of loyalty from a God to us, the followers of
Odin.

Meditate on **Thurisaz**, the rune of Thor. The defender of Midgard and ever
on the side of the common man.

Notes

_____

_____

_____

_____

_____

_____

_____

_____

_____

Voluspa 35

One did I see   in the wet woods bound,
A lover of ill,   and to Loki like;
By his side does Sigyn   sit, nor is glad
To see her mate: would you know yet more?

Even the trickster benefits from the strength of our societal beliefs. His mate stands by his side even though he has wronged the Gods again and again. She may not be happy with his actions or the outcome of them, but in her heart she understands a loyalty that few of us will ever comprehend in today'sthrow-away culture.

Notes

_____

_____

_____

_____

_____

_____

_____

_____

Voluspa 11
One there was born,   the best of all,
And strong was he made   with the strength of earth;
The proudest is called   the kinsman of men
Of the rulers all   throughout the world.

It is interesting to note that this brightest of the Aesir, Heimdall, born of nine mothers, would be compared to the strength of the Earth. I am sure there are all kinds of reasons why the son of nine mothers would be granted the strength of the Earth and of the ice cold sea and of the blood of swine. All are timeless measures of the primal power of nature. But our focus should be on the fact that he is the kinsman of men and kings; that blood and that strength flows within us and can always be called upon to surmount the obstacles in our lives. The seeds of our greatness are already within us.

Meditate on **Inguz** the seed of the divine with us.

Notes

Groagaldr 7
"Then next I will chant thee, if needs thou must travel,
And wander a purposeless way:
The bolts of Urth shall on every side
Be thy guards on the road thou goest."

Is it not always the desire of men to know that there is an element of the divine there to help us out along the way? We have all seen folk we know who appear to wander through life with no apparent purpose. But just as we believe there is guidance for us, perhaps our belief could be reinforced and made grander if we take Tolkien's words to heart: "Not all those who wander are lost."

Notes

_____

_____

_____

_____

_____

_____

_____

_____

_____

_____

Hovamol III
On his ring swore Othin the oath, methinks;
Who now his troth shall trust?
Suttung's betrayal   he sought with drink,
And Gunnloth to grief he left.

This is a difficult idea to deal with, the Allfather breaking his oath.
While there is a certain amount of regret and concern about who will trust
his troth again, the reason he broke it far outweighed whatever slight his
honor may have suffered. We should also take into consideration that we
cannot always ascribe human ideals to the Gods. The manner in which
they interact with lesser beings is far and away above our mental capacity
to understand. Needless to say, though, we must always do our best to
keep our word.

Meditate on **Jera** the harvest of right action

Notes
_____
_____
_____
_____
_____
_____
_____
_____
_____
_____

Hovamol 117
I rede thee, Loddfafnir!   and hear thou my rede,-
Profit thou hast if thou hearest,
Great thy gain if thou learnest:
Seek never to win   the wife of another,
Or long for her secret love.

An entire volume could be written about these last two lines. All through the Germanic lore we find stories of romantic love and love lost. Tacitus pointed out that it was one of our strongest points, the solid foundation of a relationship between a man and woman, husband and wife. Keeping our ego in check and doing our best to develop and be loyal to the relationship we have, and respecting others' attempts to do the same, is the right course of action that will pay enormous dividends throughout our lives.

Notes

Hovamol 121
I rede thee, Loddfafnir!   and hear thou my rede,-
Profit thou hast if thou hearest,
Great thy gain if thou learnest:
If a friend thou hast   whom thou fully wilt trust,
Then fare to find him oft;
For brambles grow   and waving grass
On the rarely trodden road.

If life has benefitted you with a good and true friend, make the time to appreciate them.

Meditate on **Wunjo** the rune of joy and fellowship

Notes

Hovamol 122
I rede thee, Loddfafnir!   and hear thou my rede,-
Profit thou hast if thou hearest,
Great thy gain if thou learnest:
A good man find   to hold in friendship,
And give heed to his healing charms.

We may find a refuge from grief in our wisdom, but to have a good friend for support during trying times is priceless. Sometimes all we need to find our way out of self-imposed prison is a gentle, or not so gentle, reminder from a person who knows us and whom we trust.

Notes

_____

_____

_____

_____

_____

_____

_____

_____

_____

Hovamol 123
I rede thee, Loddfafnir!   and hear thou my rede,-
Profit thou hast if thou hearest,
Great thy gain if thou learnest:
Be never the first   to break with thy friend
The bond that holds you both;
Care eats the heart   if thou canst not speak
To another all thy thought.

A true friend is hard to find; take care to work on the friendship for it can be a very lonely road when you try to go it alone.

Meditate on **Raidho**, the rune of our journey.

Notes

_____
_____
_____
_____
_____
_____
_____
_____
_____
_____

Hovamol 125
For never thou mayst   from an evil man
A good requital get;
But a good man oft   the greatest love
Through words of praise will win thee.

A demonstration of loyalty to a friend can be a powerful thing. Standing up for them, and being on their side in front of people who would discredit or lie about them, can be one of the things that make you unique to that person.

Notes

Hovamol 126
Mingled is love   when a man can speak
To another all his thought;
Nought is so bad   as false to be,
No friend speaks only fair.

It speaks volumes to me that in an age we have always perceived as brutal and tough, and full of manly men doing manly things, we find at its cultural roots, in our sagas and Eddas, a power to love built on the confidence of real men and even more powerful loyalties. Is it possible to build that kind of confidence in today's world? I firmly believe it is, and Asatru points the way.

Meditate on **Ihwaz**, the yew which our vertical axis to become all we can.

Notes
_____
_____
_____
_____
_____
_____
_____
_____
_____
_____

Groagaldr 8
"Then third I will chant thee, if threatening streams
The danger of death shall bring:
Yet to Hel shall turn both Horn and Ruth,
And before thee the waters shall fail."

In a day and age, with our magnificent bridges, when we no longer perceive the difficulty of crossing even a medium-sized stream, this passage may not at first glance seem so important. But Thor crossed rivers to get to the meeting hall of Asgard, and souls must cross rivers to enter almost every form of the afterlife in so many different religions and mythologies it's difficult to count. It is a very real concern for the living and the dead. What rivers do we have to cross in our lives today? What events are unfolding around us that could sweep us off our path? Do not fear them. Persevere and believe.

Notes

_____

_____

_____

_____

_____

_____

_____

_____

_____

_____

Skirnismol 5
Skirnir spake:
"Thy longings, methinks,   are not so large
That thou mayst not tell them to me;
Since in days of yore   we were young together,
We two might each other trust."

A long and trusted friendship will not encounter a trial it cannot overcome. Skadi, and some say Njord, sent Skirnir to visit with Frey to determine what the matter could be, why was he so sullen. Thus began a long and rewarding journey for Skirnir on Frey's behalf to win him the hand of Gerd.

Meditate on **Ehwaz** the rune of teamwork symbolized by the horse

Notes
_____
_____
_____
_____
_____
_____
_____
_____
_____
_____

Vafthruthnismol 1
"Counsel me, Frigg,   for I long to fare,
And Vafthruthnir fain would find;
In wisdom old   with the giant wise
Myself would I seek to match."

What a pleasant surprise when we find Odin treating as an equal, and asking the opinion of, his loyal partner Frigga. It speaks to me at some level to know this is possible between partners. We see such a loyal, trusting exchange between the mightiest of the Aesir. It also reminds us that Frigga possesses as much foreknowledge as Odin.

Notes

Groagaldr 9
"Then fourth I will chant thee, if come thy foes
On the gallows-way against thee:
Into thine hands shall their hearts be given,
And peace shall the warriors wish."

In the world of men throughout history we can count on just a few things.
Unfortunately one of the ugliest is that men will be cruel to other men.
Many religions require scapegoats to whom they are cruel in order to
promote themselves. What a reassuring sign that we can all believe in,
that a mother always wants the best for her child and protection from the
evils of other men.

Meditate on *Issa* the rune of ice, to slow things down and concentrate.

Notes
_____
_____
_____
_____
_____
_____
_____
_____
_____
_____

Groagaldr 15
"Now fare on the way where danger waits,
Let evils not lessen thy love!
I have stood at the door of the earth-fixed stones,
The while I chanted thee charms."

Our ancestors are with us, death has not lessened their love for us, and as for myself I will never doubt them.

Notes

_____

_____

_____

_____

_____

_____

_____

_____

_____

_____

Kormac's Saga
"When the wolf of the war-god was howling
Erstwhile in the north, thou didst aid me:
When it gaped in my hand, and it girded
At the Valkyries' gate for to enter.
But now wilt thou never, O warrior,
At need in the storm-cloud of Odin
Give me help in the tempest of targes
- Untrusty, unfaithful art thou."

It is to be regretted that life moves in such a manner that old friends, once engaged against magnificent foes, lose or break their bonds as time goes on. This is a very real challenge in today's society. As everyone wants to head to the top of the corporate ladder, don't sacrifice loyal friends to do it. That doesn't mean they won't do it to you, but you get the chance to sleep well at night having lived by solid principles.

Meditate on **Sowilo** the sun rune and a symbol of success.

Notes
_____
_____
_____
_____
_____
_____
_____
_____
_____
_____

Heimskringla
...but in
spring he set out leaving Driva behind, and although he had
promised to return within three years he did not come back for
ten.

There is so much more riding on your ability to keep your word than just
your honor. In this case it was a man's life.

Notes

Heimskringla
"Jorund has travelled far and wide,
But the same horse he must bestride
On which he made brave Gudlog ride.
He too must for a necklace wear
Hagbert's fell noose in middle air.
The army leader thus must ride
On Horva's horse, at Lymfjord's side."

One should never underestimate the resolve of an aggrieved son.

Meditate on **Tiwaz** a rune for justice

Notes

_____

_____

_____

_____

_____

_____

_____

_____

_____

_____

Laxdaela Saga

So she had a ship built secretly in a wood, and when it was ready built she arrayed it, and had great wealth withal; and she took with her all her kinsfolk who were left alive; and men deem that scarce may an example be found that any one, a woman only, has ever got out of such a state of war with so much wealth and so great a following. From this it may be seen how peerless among women she was. Unn had with her many men of great worth and high birth.

Loyalty flows both ways: when it is given, it is received. This endeavor by Unn the Deepminded is a fine demonstration of loyalty to her kin and the success that loyalty brought her.

Notes

_____

_____

_____

_____

_____

_____

_____

_____

_____

_____

Prose Edda
There are many fair places in heaven, and over everything there a godlike
watch is kept.

Rest your backs awhile under the shade of Yggdrasil, gaze upon the
wonders of our heavens, and with this image in your heart, turn strong
and meet the day.

Meditate on **Laguz** the powerful waters of the ocean.

Notes
_____
_____
_____
_____
_____
_____
_____
_____
_____

Prose Edda

Hárr answered: "A wise man would not ask thus, seeing that all are able to tell this; but if thou alone art become so slight of understanding as not to have heard it, then I will yet permit that thou shouldst rather ask foolishly once, than that thou shouldst be kept longer in ignorance of a thing which it is proper to know. He is called Svásudr who is father of Summer; and he is of pleasant nature, so that from his name whatsoever is pleasant is called 'sweet.'"

Ask those things that you would ask. Learn those things we ought to know. Certain stories are repeated in the Eddas for a reason. There is a much deeper understanding to be had from this body of literature and our faith than many of us are prepared to handle. Ask and learn even if it is difficult.

Notes
_____
_____
_____
_____
_____
_____
_____
_____
_____

Prose Edda
"Odin is highest and eldest of the Æsir: he rules all things, and mighty as
are the other gods, they all serve him as children obey a father."

All of our deities – the mighty Thor, valiant Tyr, watchfull Heimdall –
bear allegiance and loyalty to Odin. We can do no less than follow their
fine example.

Meditate on **Perthro** the rune of the lot cup

Notes

_____

_____

_____

_____

_____

_____

_____

_____

_____

Prose Edda

Odin is called Allfather because he is father of all the gods. He is also called Father of the Slain, because all those that fall in battle are the sons of his adoption; for them he appoints Valhalla and Vingólf, and they are then called Champions.

There is a place for the loyal and brave to assist the Gods in their endeavors. Our place is determined by our actions. Live a life of worth.

Notes

_____

_____

_____

_____

_____

_____

_____

_____

_____

Prose Edda
But no one is so wise that he can tell all his mighty works; yet I can tell thee so much tidings of him that the hours would be spent before all that I know were told.

Speaking of mighty works, we know that a great many were done on our behalf. Thor, the product of a union between earth and sky, has ever stood on our side and is our protector. His loyalty to us is repeatedly demonstrated. Let us not falter when the time comes to demonstrate ours to him. Hail Thor!

Meditate on **Thurisaz** the rune of Thor.

Notes
_____
_____
_____
_____
_____
_____
_____
_____
_____

Honsa-Thori's Saga

Blund-Ketil said, I recognize the man now from what you told me, because I was with his father when I was younger. I never met a more honorable man than his father. Now it is unfortunate that his son is in such difficulties, and his father will expect me to give him some help if he needs it. Tomorrow morning early you ride out to the harbor and invite him here with as many men as he wants. If he would rather stay somewhere else, I'll transport him wherever he wishes, north or south. I'll try my best to help him out.

This is an example of loyalty to the son of an honorable man, and the willingness to back up that sentiment with action. I try my best to do the same thing, and it has created a larger world for me.

Notes

_____

_____

_____

_____

_____

_____

_____

_____

_____

_____

Egil's Saga
Arinbjorn and Egil parted in love and friendship. Arinbjorn went to seek
Eric's sons, and joined the company of Harold Gray-fell his foster-son,
and was with him henceforth so long as they both lived.

It takes true confidence to be able to express thoughts and ideals that our
modern society has deemed effeminate, while maintaining our own
masculinity. What we should keep in mind is that these men have gone a
harrying and would likely cut someone's head off if they were laughed at.

Meditate on **Wunjo**, the joy of fellowship

Notes
_____
_____
_____
_____
_____
_____
_____
_____
_____
_____

Egil's Saga
Runes none should grave ever
Who knows not to read them;
Of dark spell full many
The meaning may miss.
Ten spell-words writ wrongly
On whale-bone were graven:
Whence to leek-tending maiden,
Long sorrow and pain.

This is the third time I've found a description of the runes and their use. Odin tells of them, Brunhilde tells Sigurth of them, and here we see Egil put them into use, to remove a curse and offer healing with them. It is no accident that in all the various mythologies and religions the world over, harmony with the forces around us is achieved with a spoken word. A wavelength of sound to complement all the other wavelengths we still strive to understand. All energy is measured in waves – from light to sound to earthquakes and brain patterns. The runes offer us a way to align our thoughts and actions with these waves; we cannot change them but we may more closely align ourselves with the good inherent in them.

Notes

_____

_____

_____

_____

_____

_____

_____

_____

_____

_____

Egil's Saga

Egil made him ready early next morning to continue his journey, as did his comrades, but at parting Egil gave Alf a fur cloak. Alf took the gift with thanks, saying, 'A good mantle have I here.' And he bade Egil visit him on the way back. They parted friends.

A simple exchange of gifts, if it comes from the heart, is often sufficient to warm the relations between the most difficult of men.

Meditate on **Gebo** the gift rune.

Notes

_____

_____

_____

_____

_____

_____

_____

_____

_____

_____

Laxdaela Saga
So Thorgerd married Herjolf, and went with him to his home, and they loved each other dearly. Thorgerd soon showed by her ways that she was a woman of the greatest mettle, and Herjolf's manner of life was deemed much better and more highly to be honored now that he had got such a one as she was for his wife.

Here we have the most romantic form of loyalty: the loyalty to each other. What finer way to build something of worth and beauty, than to embrace the loyalty to and love for one another and raise children in a home that values this bond.

Notes

_____

_____

_____

_____

_____

_____

_____

_____

_____

_____

Yule/ December

Wisdom
_____

Prose Edda
The gods had a dispute with the folk which are called Vanir, and they appointed a peace-meeting between them and established peace in this way: they each went to a vat and spat their spittle therein. Then at parting the gods took that peace-token and would not let it perish, but shaped thereof a man. This man is called Kvasir, and he was so wise that none could question him concerning anything but that he knew the solution. He went up and down the earth to give instruction to men.

This ancient tale tells us that the Gods brokered peace among themselves and used that hard-won peace to better mankind, to provide for us guidance on how to avoid difficulties. Our Gods have shown compassion and caring for us again and again. It is our destiny to rise from this learning, and to develop into beings worthy of ascending to their side.

Meditate on **Othala** our ancestral lot.

Notes

Prose Edda

When he came to the hall-door, the Æsir invited him to drink. He went within and ordered drink to be brought to him, and then those flagons were brought in from which Thor was wont to drink; and Hrungnir swilled from each in turn. But when he had become drunken, then big words were not wanting: he boasted that he would lift up Valhalla and carry it to Jotunheim, and sink Asgard and kill all the gods, save that he would take Freyja and Sif home with him.

A most offensive passage to be sure: the threats of a drunken boor never sit well with any folk. But if we are honest with ourselves can we see where we have been selfish in a similar manner, creating a heaven for ourselves and taking the harvest and love with us, not wanting to share it, maybe even killing to keep from sharing it. The fact that a jotun is making these obnoxious claims is merely a representation of man demanding that which he is not prepared for in his drunken state, pipe dreams if you will. Asatru is a way of life; it is not something we can simply sit around and proclaim our greatness with, unless we have put the Nine Noble Virtues into effect in our daily lives. Once we begin to live it, these things are given and become available to us freely.

Notes

Prose Edda

When he came upon invitation to the abode of certain dwarves, Fjalar and
Galarr, they called him into privy converse with them, and killed him,
letting his blood run into two vats and a kettle. The kettle is named
Ódrerir, and the vats Son and Bodn; they blended honey with the blood,
and the outcome was that mead by the virtue of which he who drinks
becomes a skald or scholar. The dwarves reported to the Æsir that Kvasir
had choked on his own shrewdness, since there was none so wise there as
to be able to question his wisdom.

There is a recurring theme in the Eddas of individuals attempting to
garner for themselves wisdom and learning, which they think they are
ready for, when actually they are not. There are no shortcuts for such
creatures. They are of the night and have no business showing themselves
in, nor indeed can they handle, the sunlight. Most often they are turned to
stone. Even with all their learning they cannot implement enlightenment
in their lives. People are much the same way. We have to learn by
example. We need to see the success of it. Odin worked hard to reclaim
this gift the Gods set before us. But only a few chosen of us have what it
takes to share this wisdom. We have a responsibility to demonstrate this
to the rest.

Meditate on **Sowilo** the run of the sun

Notes

359

Hovamol 6
A man shall not boast   of his keenness of mind,
But keep it close in his breast;
To the silent and wise   does ill come seldom
When he goes as guest to a house;
(For a faster friend   one never finds
Than wisdom tried and true.)

This old stanza can best be summed up in the words of Benjamin Franklin:"It is better to keep your mouth closed and let people assume you are an idiot, than to open your mouth and remove all doubt." In today's atmosphere, where ever more radical ideologiesare becoming the accepted norm for our actions, as Asatruars we have got to act in accordance with our ideals. Sitting around talking about it will not make your world a better place. Try harder today.

Notes
_____
_____
_____
_____
_____
_____
_____
_____
_____

Hovamol 7
The knowing guest   who goes to the feast,
In silent attention sits;
With his ears he hears,   with his eyes he watches,
Thus wary are wise men all.

"The knowing guest" I take to be someone who has a little knowledge of whom he will be dealing with. With that knowledge he can approach the situation with an open mind and learn from his associates. There is no daydreaming; in silent attention the knowing guest sits, giving rapt attention and taking the time to earn wisdom, for it does not always come to the individual by way of some large crisis or personal suffering. The most beautiful lessons can be learned at the arm of an elderly dinner guest.

Meditate on **Issa**, slow thing sown and concentrate like the ice on a river.

Notes

_____

_____

_____

_____

_____

_____

_____

_____

_____

Hovamol 8
Happy the one who wins for himself
Favor and praises fair;
Less safe by far is the wisdom found
That is hid in another's heart.

Do not rely on others' perceptions of you to determine who you are
supposed to be.

Notes

Hovamol 9
Happy the man who has while he lives
Wisdom and praise as well,
For evil counsel a man full oft
Has from another's heart.

If you can do your best to apply the Nine Noble Virtues in your life on a daily basis, your name and fame will grow of its own accord. Try your best never to be distracted by what another thinks you should be doing.

Meditate on **Kenaz** the torch of knowledge.

Notes
_____
_____
_____
_____
_____
_____
_____
_____
_____
_____

Hovamol 10
A better burden   may no man bear
For wanderings wide than wisdom;
It is better than wealth   on unknown ways,
And in grief a refuge it gives.

Traveling through life is a wandering adventure all its own. We will encounter countless people, places, things, and situations as we go. If we can positively build upon each experience, guided by our faith in Asatru, then when the time comes and the lessons of life are at their toughest, our wisdom and understanding of ourselves and the world we live in will aid us in getting through it.

Notes

_____

_____

_____

_____

_____

_____

_____

_____

_____

_____

Hovamol 14
Drunk I was,   I was dead-drunk,
When with Fjalar wise I was:
'Tis the best of drinking if back one brings,
His wisdom with him home.

This could be construed as a justification for indulging in binge drinking with the goal of coming away from it looking smart. This is very difficult to do. We should first consider who Odin is referring to when he made this statement – that being Fjalar the dwarf, who helped make the mead of inspiration from the blood of Kvasir. Now we can see that Odin is making rightful claim to being the source of inspiration for scholars and bards, as he has had the best of drinking and brought his wisdom home with him. This is where we should look for wisdom and guidance, the Allfather himself, not the bottom of a bottle.

Meditate on **Ansuz** the rune of Odin and the estatic state of inspiration.

Notes

Hovamol 15
The son of a king   shall be silent and wise,
And bold in battle as well;
Bravely and gladly   a man shall go,
Till the day of his death is come.

These simple, straightforward statements are given as fact, without any kind of flowery presentation, about the manner in which we are expected to live our lives. This reinforces the very simple tenet that life is good; once we have a handle on that, everything else just kind of falls into place.

Notes

_____

_____

_____

_____

_____

_____

_____

_____

_____

Hovamol 22
A paltry man   and poor of mind
At all things ever mocks;
For never he knows,   what he ought to know,
That he is not free from faults.

If we sit around talking about other people it takes away an awful lot of time we ought to be using to improve ourselves.

Meditate on **Ihwaz**, the yew our vertical axis of growth.

Notes

_____

_____

_____

_____

_____

_____

_____

_____

_____

_____

Hovamol 23
The witless man   is awake all night,
Thinking of many things;
Care-worn he is   when the morning comes,
And his woe is just as it was.

I've seen this and wondered, "Just howcanI quit worrying about this or that?" I've found it helps to get it in perspective and realize that the label of good or bad is something I've put on the situation;then I can do my best to understand that whatever it is, no matter what is going on, it is simply a part of the process of life. Once I can yield to the much greater forces at work and let them do their thing – using my talents, strengths and abilities as best as I can in each and every situation – then I can go bravely and gladly to the day of my death.

Notes
_____
_____
_____
_____
_____
_____
_____
_____
_____

Hovamol 24
The foolish man   for friends all those
        Who laugh at him will hold;
When among the wise   he marks it not
        Though hatred of him they speak.

Not everyone you meet will be your friend. This does not mean we should
not deal with them in an open and friendly manner, but don't trust
everyone you meet at work or on the street to come to your defense if you
need it. We should always be aware that the countless experiences other
people have gone through may not have been the catalysts they should've
been for them to grow.

Meditate on **Mannaz**, the rune of mankind.

Notes

Hovamol 25
The foolish man   for friends all those
Who laugh at him will hold;
But the truth when he comes   to the council he learns,
That few in his favour will speak.

As per the previous stanza we should be aware that other people may view us with disdain when they take our inventory and judge us for who we are and what we are doing, although they do not say so to our faces. Do not count on such false friends to take a stand in your defense. We cannot be all things to all people, but I can be the best "me" I can be. Avoiding leading with the chin will help us achieve that and avoid a victim mentality.

Notes

_____

_____

_____

_____

_____

_____

_____

_____

_____

Hovamol 26
An ignorant man   thinks that all he knows,
When he sits by himself in a corner;
But never what answer   to make he knows,
When others with questions come.

The armchair quarterbacks of life lack courage. When it comes time to speak your mind intelligently about a subject, or to take action and implement an idea, make sure you've done the homework and prepared yourself for such an occasion. How many times has someone we held in high regard – either a personal acquaintance or a public figure we've seen on TV – let us down when faced with the opportunity to actually implement all the great things we've believed they have said? Then we realize that perhaps we really should have looked at both sides of the coin. Don't be an ignorant man.

Meditate on **Raidho**, the journey of life.

Notes
_____
_____
_____
_____
_____
_____
_____
_____
_____
_____

Hovamol 27
A witless man,   when he meets with men,
Had best in silence abide;
For no one shall find   that nothing he knows,
If his mouth is not open too much.
(But a man knows not, if nothing he knows,
When his mouth is open too much.)

Oddly enough, some folk have a very difficult time accepting the fact that there are other people better than them. It is a simple and plain fact that some people are further along the road in life than we are. I am not as strong as Arnold, nor can I fight like Vladimir Klitchko, and my ability to handle money pales in comparison to Warren Buffet's. The last thing I need to do is enter a conversation with any of them pretending I have any kind of insight into their respective subject matters. In those situations I need to keep my mouth shut.

Notes

_____

_____

_____

_____

_____

_____

_____

_____

_____

_____

Hovamol 28
Wise shall he seem   who well can question,
        And also answer well;
Nought is concealed   that men may say
        Among the sons of men.

If we can begin to know ourselves and seek self-improvement, we will have made a fine beginning in enacting this stanza in our lives. Once we begin to understand ourselves, our limitations and strengths, without an overbearing ego in the way, we will thirst for knowledge. We will be able to ask the intelligent question of those who know things we do not, without trying to impress them with our own knowledge. We will be able to think clearly for ourselves and reply with an answer that does not seek to make ourselves seem more than we are. People will notice this and share it with others.

Meditate on **Dagaz** the dawn and awakening to life.

Notes

_____

_____

_____

_____

_____

_____

_____

_____

_____

_____

Hovamol 29
Often he speaks   who never is still
With words that win no faith;
The babbling tongue, if a bridle it find not,
Oft for itself sings ill.

I have met and worked with several individuals who avoid silence as
much as they can. Their ceaseless prattle carries on and on until such
time as they find a subject that generates a response. Typically among
such folk this subject is never a big idea; most likely it will be about
themselves and some situation in their lives. It is a curious phenomenon
that people will gossip. Once they've gotten the dirt on someone, from the
horse's mouth as it were, it spreads, and those talkative people begin to
wonder: How did this happen, how can everyone know, why does
everyone look at me like that? Their own babbling tongue has sown the
very seeds of their destruction.

Notes
_____
_____
_____
_____
_____
_____
_____
_____
_____
_____

Hovamol 30
In mockery no one a man shall hold,
Although he fare to the feast;
Wise seems one oft,   if nought he is asked,
And safely he sits dry-skinned.

In Asatru I have found many reasons to be comfortable with myself. In assuming that attitude I find it much easier to sit among friends and associates, listening and learning instead of yammering to draw attention to myself and seem more important than I really am. In developing confidence in myself, and in understanding who I am and my relation to the Gods and the world around me, I find peace and security.

Meditate on **Berkano** a rune of renewal.

Notes

Hovamol 31
Wise a guest holds it to take to his heels,
When mock of another he makes;
But little he knows who laughs at the feast,
Though he mocks in the midst of his foes.

It's hard to be taken seriously when making fun of another person or complaining about them if you have a booger on your shirt. Think twice before you try to build yourself up at another's expense, for who really knows how others perceive you.

Notes

Hovamol 56
A measure of wisdom each man shall have
But never too much let him know;
Let no man the fate   before him see,
For so is he freest from sorrow.

Perhaps it is a gift that we cannot see the future; in our ignorance we get to enjoy a little suffering and a little love, a little of everything in life. A brave man should embrace life, with courage. Sometimes things will cause us what seems to be an inordinate amount of pain, but we cannot shy away from them or we will shortchange ourselves and the development of who we are supposed to become. Once you begin to accept life as it comes, you will begin to enjoy a measure of contentment. You will be able to truly enjoy your wisdom and use it as refuge from sorrow.

Meditate on **Uruz** the rune of primal power.

Notes

Hovamol 122-123

122. I rede thee, Loddfafnir! | and hear thou my rede,--
Profit thou hast if thou hearest,
Great thy gain if thou learnest:
Exchange of words | with a witless ape
Thou must not ever make.

123. For never thou mayst | from an evil man
A good requital get;
But a good man oft | the greatest love
Through words of praise will win thee.

There is a particular truth to this for those of us who follow Asatru. We are surrounded by 2000 years of Christian domination of the world around us. A totalitarian religion will eventually lead to a totalitarian government. It always has. Christian influence has been insinuated into every nook and cranny of our society and other societies around the world. These fools are not people to argue with. Many of us now in Asatru have been called to this world-view in one way or another. It is such an alien and fearful thought to the majority of people to realize we may depend upon ourselves, that we may as well be speaking Greek to them. There is no more important arena than our dealings with the world in which to realize that we are our deeds. The support and encouragement we offer other Asatruar will garner a close-knit community of friends, most likely much larger than we could have hoped for.

Notes

_____

_____

_____

_____

_____

_____

_____

_____

_____

Hovamol 55
A measure of wisdom each man shall have,
But never too much let him know;
For the wise man's heart is seldom happy,
If wisdom too great he has won.

It's a funny thing about advice that wise men don't need it and fools won't heed it. A wise man's heart must sometimes witness with sadness the mistakes of his descendants. In Asatru we believe that we are our deeds. What worse torment must there be than to know beforehand that a situation will turn out badly? Even so, we must all be able to share our wisdom when a situation does go badly for our children. More importantly we have the responsibility to teach the next generation properly so as to avoid the pitfalls in life.

Meditate on *Jera* the harvest of right action.

Notes

Hovamol 89
Hope not too surely | for early harvest,
Nor trust too soon in thy son;
The field needs good weather, | the son needs wisdom,
And oft is either denied.

A good harvest and a good son require lots of effort. It requires your best effort; there really is no room for error. Ideas and seeds must be planted and cared for, nurtured to the best of your ability. If you've done your best, and the fields have been well taken care of, and your example as a man in Asatru has been the best you can possibly deliver, then perhaps, just maybe, your son and your crops will be able to weather the outside influences each will be subject to.

Notes

Hovamol 68
Fire for men   is the fairest gift,
And power to see the sun;
Health as well,   if a man may have it,
And a life not stained with sin.

If a man has all of these in his life, he has a good, good life.

Meditate on **Fehu** the rune of luck and wealth.

Notes

Hovamol 70

71. (70) It is better to live than lie like a corpse,
The live man catches the cow;
I saw flames rise for the rich man's pyre,
And before his door he lay dead.

Always keep in mind that now is the time to live, while we are here. We do not piddle away the days waiting for a kingdom after we die. Our struggles and growth here will help determine how well we can align ourselves with the mission of the Gods after we have passed through the veil. But today we are alive and a part of the wonders of nature; enjoy it.

Notes

_____

_____

_____

_____

_____

_____

_____

_____

_____

Hovamol 78
Among Fitjung's sons saw I well-stocked folds,-
Now bear they the beggar's staff;
Wealth is as swift as a winking eye,
Of friends the falsest it is.

Money isn't everything; it's only good for spending, and is only worth anything when there is something we need or want that it can buy. There are thousands of little sayings about money and they are probably all true. We are each of us in Asatru the probable possessors of a mighty heritage, and we should do our best to lay claim to it, but that does not mean we will become wealthy overnight. If our efforts within this faith are true, we can build a wealth of friends that is worth far more than any dollar amount.

Meditate on **Perthro**, the lot cup

Notes

_____

_____

_____

_____

_____

_____

_____

_____

_____

_____

Hovamol 80
Certain is that which is sought from runes,
That the gods so great have made,
And the Master-Poet painted;
Silence is safest and best.

Within the runes we may find the keys to our universe. They can be considered almost as holy as the Gods themselves, and are so considered by some folk. This is just one more aspect of the many facets of Asatru that enable us to be a part of the universe around us instead of being dominated by it.

Notes
_____
_____
_____
_____
_____
_____
_____
_____
_____
_____

| 29 | Yule |

Hovamol 79
An unwise man,   if a maiden's love
Or wealth he chances to win,
His pride will wax,   but his wisdom never,
Straight forward he fares in conceit.

Here are two fine examples of the things in life most people believe make them important – the trophy wife or a fat wallet or both. Yet time and again I've heard on TV or the radio that people who have achieved this kind of success, who walk around feeling so much more important than those around them, also feel like they have hollow empty lives. They do. I seriously doubt that the Gods put us here to live a life filled with such hollow pursuits. Yet we see so many of our family and friends tied up in this rat race, faring straight forward in their conceit.

Meditate on **Nauthiz**, the need fire.

Notes

385

Hovamol 81

Give praise to the day at evening,   to a woman on her pyre,
To a weapon which is tried,   to a maid at wedlock,
To ice when it is crossed,   to ale that is drunk.

These seemingly simple things – the day, a woman, a weapon, and so on – at first glance appear to be the solid things upon which simple men may base a good life. But only after such things have been put to good use may we trust them, not before. Each item represents many things which can make a life full and whole, or can cause seemingly unbearable pain and suffering. Do not rush in leading with the chin. Be grateful when it becomes what it's supposed to be.

Notes
_____
_____
_____
_____
_____
_____
_____
_____
_____
_____

Hovamol 74
He welcomes the night   whose fare is enough,
(Short are the yards of a ship,)
Uneasy are autumn nights;
Full oft does the weather change in a week,
And more in a month's time.

Tired and in need of rest at the end of hard days' work; focused on the task at hand – usually repetitive in nature – to get the desired result and provide for our family; if we have done our best when autumn comes and the harvest is at hand or already in and the food stores are prepared for winter, all will be well. So we welcome the night as we have done our best, and we give praise to the Gods, welcoming their blessing into our lives.

Meditate on *Jera* the harvest of right action.

Notes
_____
_____
_____
_____
_____
_____
_____
_____
_____
_____

9 781500 805722